EDITOR: MARTIN WINDROW

OSPREY
MILITARY

ELITE SERIES

23

THE SAMURAI

Text by
ANTHONY BRYANT

Colour plates by
ANGUS McBRIDE

Published in 1989 by
Osprey Publishing Ltd
59 Grosvenor Street, London W1X 9DA
© Copyright 1989 Osprey Publishing Ltd
Reprinted 1991

British Library Cataloguing in Publication Data

Bryant, Anthony J.
    The Samurai. 1. Japan. Samurai, to 1868
    I. Title   II. Series
    305.5; 2

    ISBN 0-85045-897-8

Filmset in Great Britain
Printed through Bookbuilders Ltd, Hong Kong

Dedication
For the Sakuras—Steve and Kimmy Bloom—who started something big; and with affection to my friends in the SCA.

Acknowledgements
This book would not have been possible without the help and co-operation of several people, notably Yutaka Matsushita (a.k.a. Kôzan-sensei) and Tomizô Usami, owner and manager of the Tokyo armour shop *Yoroi no Kôzan-Dô* (1-23-11 Asakusabashi, Taitô-ku), who let me prowl and poke around at all hours. Also a sincere thank you to Those Who Came Before—Steve Turnbull, H. Russell Robinson, and especially to the man who may be Japan's greatest living expert on the manufacturer of armour, Yoshihiko Sasama.

Artist's Note
Readers may care to note that the original paintings from which the colour plates in this book were prepared are available for private sale. All reproduction copyright whatsoever is retained by the publisher. All enquiries should be addressed to:
    Scorpio Gallery
    P.O. Box 475
    Hailsham
    E. Sussex BN27 2SL
The publishers regret that they can enter into no correspondence upon this matter.

Errata
We regret the following minor errors, which were only detected at a late stage of production. *Plate A1*: There should be only one row of white lacing at the top, followed by one yellow, followed by the graded shades from lightest pink to deep red. *Plate A5*: The top two rows should be one purple above one red, not two red. *Plate C*: The title, as correctly given in the commentary, should be 'Ichi-no-Tani'.

The Samurai

Introduction

Who—and what—were *samurai*? Today the word has become rather over-used. Not all of the warriors of historical Japan were samurai; so it is not surprising to find that not all of the samurai were warriors. They were the upper class in a society represented by the tetragram *shi-nô-kô-shô*: warriors, farmers, artisans, and tradesmen.

They were undoubtedly a military class, but many samurai became renowned as men of letters and the arts. Most of what Europe would call 'Renaissance men' came from samurai families—those skilled with the brush as well as the sword, the flute as well as the bow. With the exception of the court aristocracy, few of those born outside the samurai class could ever aspire to achieve fame or recognition in any area of endeavour.

The term *samurai* comes from the obsolete verb *saburau*, which means 'to serve'. *Saburau* could be taken to mean 'to serve' in the same sense that today we speak of serving in the army, as well as in the more common sense of, e.g., a household servant.

Bushi is a term virtually interchangeable with the word samurai; in fact, it is an older term, first appearing in the Nara Era (710–784), pre-dating the first usage of 'samurai' by several centuries. (An older, obsolete term, *mononofu*, was used during the ancient period.) Bushi refers to those who fight; in fact the second character (*shi*) can be read 'samurai'.

Still another term was applied to the warrior caste in medieval Japan: *ji-samurai*. This referred strictly to those samurai from powerful families, usually those unallied or unconnected to the *bakufu*, the military government in Kamakura. This term was in widest use around the latter half of the Muromachi Period (15th–16th centuries).

Throughout this text, the terms 'bushi' and 'samurai' will be used interchangeably. In writings of the period, the term bushi would appear to have been in more common use within the ranks in reference to their own class.

One note for the reading of this book: names have been left in Japanese order, surname first, given name last.

This model is wearing an *ô-yoroi* in the style and fashion of the 13th century, contemporary with the Mongol invasions. Note that he only wears a single *kote*.

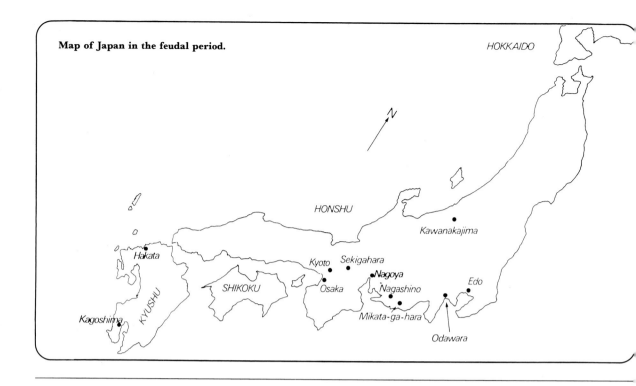

Map of Japan in the feudal period.

HOKKAIDO

HONSHU

Kawanakajima

Hakata

Kyoto Sekigahara

Nagoya

SHIKOKU Osaka Nagashino Edo

KYUSHU

Mikata-ga-hara

Kagoshima

Odawara

Chronology

935–40 Taira no Masakado claims title of New Emperor, fails in revolt against legitimate Imperial line.

1028–31 Failed rebellion of Taira no Tadatsune in Shimofusa.

1051–62 Early Nine Year's War: Abe no Yoritoki rebels, crushed by Minamoto no Yoriyoshi.

1083–87 Later Three Years' War: Kiyohara no Iehira (Governor of Mutsu) rebels, crushed by Minamoto no Yoshiie.

1156 Hôgen Insurrection: ex-emperor Sutoku opposes Emperor Go-Shirakawa; rise of Taira no Kiyomori.

1159 Heiji Insurrection: Minamoto no Yoshitomo fails to overthrow Taira no Kiyomori.

1180–85 Genpei War: the Minamoto (Genji) overthrow the Taira (Heike). 1181 Prince Mochihito killed; 1183 Yoshinaka enters Kyôto; 1184 battle of Ichi-no-Tani; 1185 Taira annihilated at Dan-no-Ura.

1192 Minamoto no Yoritomo becomes first of the Kamakura-based shôgun, opens Kamakura *bakufu*.

1203 Hiki Rebellion: Minamoto no Yoriie fails to overthrow the Hôjô.

1221 Jôkyû Upheaval: ex-emperor Go-Toba fails to end the power of the Hôjô shôgunal regency.

1274 First Mongol invasion of Kyûshû fails.

1281 Second Mongol invasion of Kyûshû; the *kami-kaze* destroys the invading fleet.

1324 Shôchû Upheaval: ex-emperor Go-Daigo fails to overthrow the Kamakura bakufu.

1333 Ashikaga Takauji et al. overthrow the bakufu. Imperial rule restored.

1336 Battle of Minatogawa. Takauji defeats Yoshisada and Masashige. Takauji proclaims new emperor and becomes first Ashikaga shôgun, opening the Muromachi bakufu and Period (to 1573). Go-Daigo forms own Imperial Court in Yoshino. Beginning of the *Nanboku-chô Senso*

Origins and Rise of the Warrior Class

It is tempting to wonder to what extent Buddhism caused the rise of the effete and ineffectual court life, and to what extent it was due to the Chinese. Before the advent of Chinese influence and Buddhist teachings, the Imperial line was much more involved in the actual day-to-day running of the country, the emperor himself having been known to lead armies into battle.

One of the greatest early warrior-heroes was Imperial Prince Yamato, a combination of Roland and Galahad, with a bit of St George added for good measure; another was the Empress Jingô, who led an invasion of Korea while pregnant. Her son became the Emperor Ojin; he was deified after his death as the war god Hachiman. Such was the Imperial line before AD 550.

After the Sino-Buddhist arrival in the early 6th century, there was a struggle between the supporters of Shintô (the native religion) and those of the imported Buddhism before the latter prevailed. During this time Japan also began a period of Sinification, when the writing system, costume, and architecture of China had a profound influence. Chinese court bureaucracy was also copied; and since Japen had, for the time being, sufficiently subdued the barbarians in the north, this perhaps compounded the decline of the emperor's practical powers.

Court politics were dominated by the powerful Fujiwara family, who managed to marry many daughters into the Imperial line. The emperor became more and more reclusive, partly due to the machinations of the Fujiwara. (At one point, a Fujiwara minister actually had to issue an order for labourers to work the soil in the Imperial Presence so that the emperor would understand what 'field

	(War of the Northern and Southern Courts).	**1575**	Battle of Nagashino. Using guns, Nobunaga and Tokugawa Ieyasu defeat Takeda Katsuyori.
1392	Capitulation of the legitimate Southern Imperial line.	**1582**	Akechi Mitsuhide rebels and assassinates Nobunaga. Hashiba (later Toyotomi) Hideyoshi subsequently kills Mitsuhide.
1426	*Ikki* uprisings reach Kyôto.		
1467–77	Onin War: family squabble leads to dispute for shôgunal succession and war; Kyôto nearly destroyed.	**1583**	Battle of Shizugatake. Hideyoshi defeats Shibata Katsuie.
1488	In Kaga, militant Buddhist *Ikkô-Ikki* take over the whole province. Domination lasts until 1570s.	**1584**	Battle of Komaki-Nagakute. Hideyoshi and Ieyasu fight to a stalemate.
		1585	Hideyoshi becomes *kanpaku*; makes peace with Ieyasu.
1495	Rise of Hôjô Sôun, first of the 'Sengoku Daimyô'.	**1590**	Hideyoshi virtually completes his subjugation of Japan with conquest of northern Honshû.
1542	Portuguese land at Tanegashima. Firearms are introduced into Japan.		
1555	First battle at Kawanakajima between Takeda Shingen and Uesugi Kenshin.	**1592**	Hideyoshi dispatches first army to Korea.
		1597	Second army dispatched to Korea.
1560	Battle of Okehazama. Oda Nobunaga, leading a small force, defeats and kills Imagawa Yoshimoto.	**1598**	Hideyoshi dies, leaving five-year-old heir.
1568	Nobunaga has Ashikaga Yoshiaki made shôgun.	**1600**	Battle of Sekigahara. Ieyasu defeats the supporters of Hideyoshi's successor in the largest battle ever fought in Japan. Secures Tokugawa hegemony.
1571	Nobunaga burns Enryakuji.		
1573	Nobunaga purges Yoshiaki, ending the Ashikaga bakufu; establishes his own government.		

labour' was.) They also instituted a tradition whereby still youthful and healthy emperors abdicated in favour of more easily controlled children. This was a dangerously foolish policy, as the number of unhappy, displaced, disaffected men with Imperial connections leaving Kyôto and affiliating with powerful ancient (non-Fujiwara) families was growing.

It is not surprising then, that the earliest campaigns of historical note were struggles by the noble class for access to or promotion in the Fujiwara-dominated court.

The first such shock was the Tenkei Rebellion by Taira no Masakado in 935. A member of one of the Imperially-related families living away from the capital, Masakado was refused the office of *kebiishi*, a position not unlike commander of the national police force, whose writs had the same influence as Imperial decree. He fled to his native Kantô area (now Tôkyô), proclaimed himself the new emperor, and began appointing friends and allies to court positions. In 940 Fujiwara no Hidesato, aided by Masakado's cousin, Taira no Sadamori, defeated the 'New Emperor' in battle; Masakado was killed and his head was sent to Kyôto. What is surprising about this event is that it took the central government five years to bring about the downfall of the rebel 'emperor'.

The government eventually learned, however, the value of the provincial samurai. When it needed a provincial governor by the name of Abe no Yoritoki subdued, it sent Minamoto no Yoriyoshi at

Glossary

ashigaru	lowest rank of samurai
bakufu	shôgunal government
daimyô	class of aristocracy
dô	cuirass
dô-maru	wrap-around cuirass, fastening on right
gekokujô	'low overcoming the high'—term for 15th C. peasant revolts
gekokujô-daimyô	nobles of humble origin
gusoko	full suit of armour (post-1400)
hachi	helmet bowl
haidate	apron-like thigh armour
hara-ate	breast-plate
haramaki	cuirass with back opening
hatamoto	retainers of daimyô
horo	billowing cape
ikki	militant peasant bands
jinbaori	surcoat worn over armour
kabuto	helmet
kanpaku	prime minister
kebiishi	important national office
katana	long sword, worn in belt cutting edge up
koku	measure of wealth
kote	armoured sleeves
kusazuri	tassets
kuwagata	flat, free-standing helmet crests
menpô	face armour
mon	heraldic device
naginata	halberd-like weapon—curved blade on a long shaft
ô-yoroi	box-like armour
odoshi/odoshi-ge	armour lacing
sashimono	banner worn from back of armour
seppuku	ritual suicide
shikken	regent ruling for a shôgun
shikoro	nape guard
shugo-daimyô	14th C. class of military aristocracy
sode	shoulder armour
sôhei/yamabushi	militant monks
suneate	greaves
tachi	long sword, suspended cutting edge down
tanegashima/teppô	matchlock musket
wakizashi	short sword worn in belt
yari	lance—they were never thrown.

the head of an army in what became known as the 'Early Nine Years' War' (1051–63). When the governor's replacement committed the same excesses as his defeated predecessor, Yoriyoshi's son, Yoshiie, was sent out to subdue him in the so-called 'Later Three Years' War' of 1083–87. Yoshiie's success was expensive, however, as no gratitude or reward was forthcoming from the court, and the costs of rewarding his men had to come from his own Minamoto coffers.

While the Minamoto were putting down a rebellion in the north, a second great clan, the Taira, which had already given one great villain to Japan, was rising in the south. In 1156, a brief dispute for the throne called the Hōgen Insurrection aided the rise of Taira no Kiyomori, who had backed the right horse. Through shrewd dealings with allies and enemies alike, Kiyomori was able to virtually replace the Fujiwara power bases with members of his own clan.

In the Heiji Insurrection of 1159, Minamoto no Yoshitomo (who had been the only Minamoto to side with Kiyomori during the Hōgen Insurrection) and Fujiwara no Nobuyori conspired to destroy the Taira clan after a quarrel over policy; but both were defeated and slain.

Two brief struggles were all it took to completely wrest the reins of government from the Fujiwara, a courtier family, and into the hands of the more military Taira.

Genji versus Heike

Westerners are often surprised by the frequent accounts in samurai annals of entire families being put to the sword for the transgressions of a single individual. Perhaps the reason for these massacres lies in the story of the struggles between the two rival clans, the Minamoto and the Taira. The latter were also called Heike, which is the Chinese reading for the characters 'Taira family', and the former were the Genji, or 'Minamoto clan'.

It all began in 1159, with the death of Minamoto Yoshitomo. Kiyomori, in his victory, made the error of showing mercy and sparing the lives of Yoshitomo's youngest boys. Two of these children would grow up to become Yoshitsune and Yoritomo, two of the greatest names in Japanese history, and would eventually put an end to the power of the Taira.

A very ornate ô-*boshi kabuto* of the style of the late 13th century. (**Kôzan-dô**)

In 1180 Prince Mochihito, who was enraged at being passed over for the Imperial throne in favour of Kiyomori's two-year-old grandson Antoku, conspired against the Heike with the oldest of the brothers, Yoritomo. Were Yoritomo to win the conflict, the throne would go to Mochihito. Yoritomo, titular head of the Genji, summoned the remnants of the Minamoto clan and their adherents and ancient allies from every corner of Japan and went to make war on Kiyomori, master of the land. Joining Yoritomo was his younger brother Yoshitsune, the two having grown up apart. Yoshitsune brought with him his most faithful vassals: Ise no Saburô, the Satô and Kamada brothers, and the giant warrior-monk Musashibô Benkei.

The Buddhist 'Church Militant'

Whether Benkei actually lived or not is now seldom disputed. It is certain that his exploits and size were greatly elaborated in the retelling; but even as a simple man of slightly larger-than-normal size, Benkei lived through enough adventures in the service of the young Minamoto general for a dozen lifetimes. It was a time which made men giants.

The Buddhist 'church militant' seems to have first appeared in 970, when monasteries began supporting what amounted to standing armies: bodies of fighting men used to defend the temples from raiders and in settling disputes with other monasteries. At times, intra-sect inter-monastery strife was just as bloody as any European medieval war of religion. In 1081, for example, the Fujiwara family temple of Kôfuku-ji attacked the temple of Enryaku-ji on Mt. Hiei, and Mii-dera, putting the latter temple to the torch and looting its treasury.

The origin of the militant Buddhists was probably not unlike that of Christian monastic orders in the Holy Land—the militants were not monks or priests *per se*, but men sworn to protect their order. As the temples grew in wealth and power, so did the number of *sôhei*, or warrior monks. The Tendai-sect temple on Mt. Hiei kept an army of several thousand, and between 981 and 1185 made numerous forays into Kyôto in efforts, frequently quite successful, to exert influence over the civil government. When the sôhei (also called *yamabushi*, or mountain warriors, after their position on Mt. Hiei) 'visited' Kyôto, they would often carry sacred emblems and relics which would allow them to claim sacrilege had been committed if they were attacked. Superstitious fears and strong religious beliefs both played a very strong part in the psychological make-up of Heian Japan, and conflicted with the Heike desire to destroy the power of the monastic armies.

There was very little resemblance between the sôhei and the samurai commanded by Kiyomori, however. The monasteries had a few skilled and seasoned commanders, and not a few of their number were gifted fighters, but a great percentage of their number were probably little more than organised rabble. Of course, the larger temples tended to have the better armies, and there were even times when Kiyomori was forced to refrain from taking action against the mighty Enryaku-ji.

The Heike flee Kyôto in this scene from a picture scroll relating the events of the Genpei War. Even in black and white, we may note the variation in lacing patterns. (Kunaichô-ji)

The Genpei War (1180–85)

The Genpei War gets its name from the combination of the characters for Minamoto and Taira. The rivalry between them was fierce; both were ancient families, descended from royalty, and successful in military ventures; but there was a huge difference. The Heike had close ties with the court and like the Fujiwara, had been marrying into the Imperial family. They were well known as accomplished artists and men of letters as well as warriors. The Genji, on the other hand, were rustics; and each side derided the other for their chosen lifestyles.

The monastic sôhei made a third force—sometimes for the Genji, sometimes for the Heike—and they frequently figured in the accounts of battle. One such was the Uji Bridge Battle in 1180, when sôhei from Tôdai-ji, a pro-Minamoto temple, engaged a huge force of Heike. After ripping up the planks of the bridge to defend their retreat, about 250–300 Genji-allied monks and samurai held off the attacking Heike and their allies for most of the day, until a body of Heike supporters were able to ford the river and distract the defenders (It was during this battle that a particularly brave sôhei by the name of Tajima got his reputation: Tajima the Arrow-Cutter stood on the planks of the bridge, a fine target for the Heike archers, and defended himself from arrows with his mighty *naginata*, whirling it to snap shafts in mid-flight.) In the end it was a Taira victory, despite the valiant attempts of the Genji adherents. In retaliation Kiyomori had Tôdai-ji put to the torch, and over 3,500 perished in the flames. Shortly afterwards, Kiyomori died—a result, some said, of his attack on the temple.

Mochihito's untimely death in battle nearly spelled the end of the Minamoto rebellion. Yoritomo, however, was determined not to give up until he had achieved victory. To this end he played the rôle of organiser, commander and politician, leaving the campaigning to his able brother Yoshitsune, and colourful cousin Minamoto Kisô no Yoshinaka.

Yoshinaka's wife was the famous Tomoe Gozen, herself a renowned warrior. She would often accompany Yoshinaka on campaign and into battle, equally armed and outfitted. Perhaps this was as much due to their rustic background as her enthusiasm; certainly, no Heike records speak of a Taira general's wife riding into the fray.

In 1182, after inflicting a severe defeat on the Taira, Yoshinaka became the first Minamoto to re-enter the capital; in fact, he took command of it. He appointed himself shôgun (itself an illegitimate appointment) and terrorised all of Kyôto, the Heike having fled and taken the child Emperor Antoku with them. At this point Yoshitomo began to view Yoshinaka as a potential rival, rather than an ally and kinsman. The appointment as shôgun, baseless as it was, must have greatly rankled Yoritomo; as head of the Minamoto clan, the title should have been his.

Yoritomo enlisted the help of Yoshitsune, youngest of the Genji generals, who holds a near-

With one glaring exception, this purple-laced *ô-yoroi* is fairly typical of those of the 13th century. Adding *haidate* was an Edo Era affectation born out of an unfamiliarity with older styles. The cords of the *sode* are not arranged as they would be if worn. (Kôzan-dô)

Modern painting of Yoshitsune. He is wearing a travelling hat. The armour is the one illustrated in Plate C. (Ookura Shukokan)

nearly struck the helmets of those in front. The cliff was sandy, so they slid about 120 feet. . . The sight was so terrifying that they shut their eyes.' It was an astounding rout for the Heike, who barely escaped annihilation.

They were not so lucky at Dan-no-Ura, a subsequent naval engagement where Yoshitsune's forces inflicted such a defeat that the Taira began a mass suicide. Emperor Antoku's grandmother (Kiyomori's widow) jumped into the sea carrying the young emperor, and Taira no Norimori tied an anchor around his waist before leaping overboard. Taira no Noritsune grabbed a Genji warrior in each arm and, firmly gripping them, he also leapt into the waves. Taira no Tomomori donned a second suit of armour and followed them into the swirling waters.

The Taira were utterly destroyed—which was a great loss for Japan, for among the Heike who perished were many renowned as men of culture,

mythical position in Japanese annals. This is doubtless due in part to his considerable military prowess, but also owes much to the romance and tragedy that surrounded him.

His reputation was first acquired by striking out, on his brother Yoritomo's orders, at his greatest enemy, Minamoto Kisô no Yoshinaka. Yoritomo had ensconced himself in Kamakura, and was acting as if he were already master of Japan, leaving his kinsmen to fight his battles for him. Yoshinaka was defeated, and fled with his wife and a few retainers; an ambush all but eliminated his small force, and he was killed shortly afterwards as he fled alone towards Awazu. Legend has it that his wife Tomoe Gozen killed some of the attackers, before fleeing to a temple and becoming a nun.

The Heike, meanwhile, had entrenched in an easily defended natural fortification called Ichi-no-Tani. Cliffs protected the north, and the fleet was at anchor in the harbour to the south. Knowing that the enemy would be ready for attacks from the east or west, Yoshitsune decided to lead a small shock force of 200 down the cliff face in a desperate all-or-nothing cavalry charge. Late on the night of 18 March 1184, they attacked. The charge was described thus in the *Heike Monogatari*: 'At the head of thirty horsemen, Yoshitsune rode down the cliff, the rest following. The stirrups of the men behind

This is a late Kamakura *ô-yoroi* in the collection of the Tôkyô National Museum. Note the side plate, and how the *shikoro* falls to cover the top of the *sode*. The lacing is bright red.

great refinement and learning: artists, poets and thinkers.

Yoritomo's work, however, was not yet done. Yoshitsune had entered Kyôto as a liberator, and was appointed kebiishi—the same position that had eluded Taira no Masakado about 250 years before. Yoritomo became more and more concerned over his brother's popularity. History attributes one of the major causes of the great falling-out to the jealousy of a Genji general against Yoshitsune. Whatever the reasons, Yoritomo gave orders for this younger brother's destruction. For almost five years Yoshitsune and a few vassals were hunted throughout Japan and picked off one by one before the tragic hero finally committed suicide in 1189 while the giant monk Benkei, the last surviving retainer, held off their pursuers.

In 1192 Yoritomo was proclaimed shôgun, and set about forming his new government—a military government, under a shôgun, not a civil government under a kanpaku. The Kamakura Era had been born.

The Kamakura Bakufu and Regency

In the Imperial court, the highest position attainable was that of kanpaku, which can be compared to that of a prime minister, although the kanpaku exerted much more control and enjoyed more freedom. There was a byzantine organisation of offices and ministeries under the kanpaku, so many that it was a wonder that things worked.

The establishment of the Kamakura bakufu (the name means 'tent government', as the government of the shôgun was seen as mobile and military, not locked into a city) began a slight streamlining of the political processes, taking a great deal of power away from the civil authorities and giving it to newer, military, administrations. One notable change was the virtual dissolution of the office of kebiishi. Perhaps Yoritomo remembered his brother's appointment; at any rate, he gave the authority to the local lords to keep their own justice, heralding a shift from central authority to a wider, looser system. He still wanted to keep control, but he knew that he would have to devolve some power

to keep it. Ruthless and cold as he was, he was a very capable administrator.

The emperor still ruled, but in name only. The true lord of Japan, operating behind the throne, was the puppet-master Yoritomo. This was one reason why the bakufu was established in Kamakura and not Kyôto, as it limited any potential influence from the Imperial court, and isolated the court and aristocracy. Soon the bakufu also took on the distinct appearance of a bureaucracy, with officers to observe military affairs and officials to oversee almost everything else.

Yoritomo's untimely death in a riding accident in 1199, at the age of 52, caused considerable consternation in the new government. Society was still in a state of flux, and it was a dangerous time to be without a leader. Although Yoritomo's young son Yoriie took the reigns of civil control, it was three years before he was given the title of shôgun.

Back of a *kabuto* of the Nanboku-chô Era, showing the complex pattern of cords which held the *sode* in place. The heavy central bow, called an *agemaki*, would later become a decorative item as seen here on the back of the *kabuto*.

Even then he was controlled by his mother, Masako, and her father Hôjô Tokimasa. So strong was she that Masako was called the *ama* (nun) *shôgun* (since she had entered orders on the death of Yoritomo). Tokimasa first engineered the forced abdication and encloisterment of the pitiful Yoriie, and then had him assassinated.

Tokimasa then made Yoriie's 12-year-old brother, Sanetomo, shôgun. Despite all the valiant efforts of the Genji, he would be the last Minamoto shôgun. As he was a minor, a regent was needed; and who better than his grandfather, Hôjô Tokimasa? Tokimasa created the office of *shikken*, or regent, and became the first of the puppet-masters

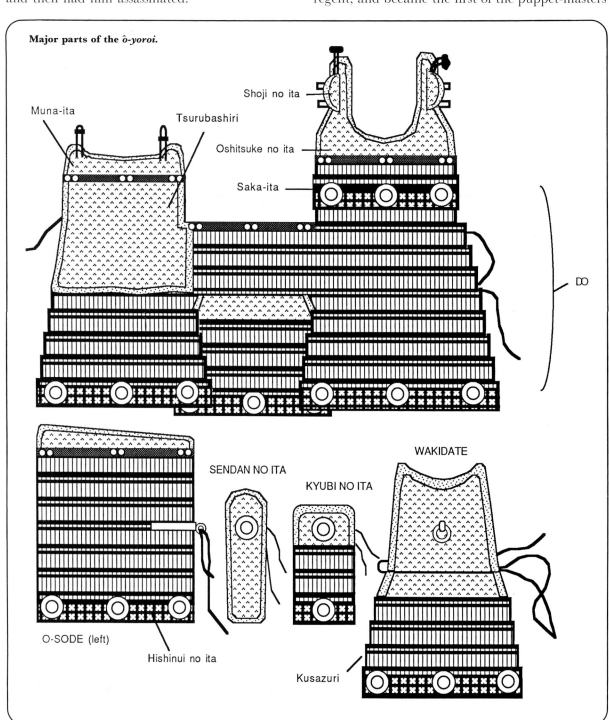

Major parts of the ô-yoroi.

Muna-ita

Tsurubashiri

Shoji no ita

Oshitsuke no ita

Saka-ita

DO

SENDAN NO ITA

KYUBI NO ITA

WAKIDATE

O-SODE (left)

Hishinui no ita

Kusazuri

to the puppet-masters. At the age of 26, the shôgun was assassinated.

Well-placed accusations of guilt laid by the shikken soon robbed Japan of Minamoto candidates for the office of shôgun; so the Hôjô shikken requested the retired Emperor Go-Toba to name one. The shikken wanted someone malleable; but Go-Toba refused to commit himself for years, while he searched for a candidate who could help him reassert Imperial power. It became a power struggle between the regent and the emperor, neither accepting the nominations of the other.

In 1221 Go-Toba finally tired of these delaying tactics; proclaimed the current regent, Hôjô Yoshitoki, to be an outlaw; and declared that a state of rebellion existed—but he was careful to indicate that his revolt was not against the bakufu. Rather, the shikken and the bakufu were in rebellion, and were guilty of running a competing government at odds with the divine Imperial line.

Go-Toba called for help from the sôhei of Enryaku-ji to support his 'righteous' cause, but none came. There were a few battles and small-scale skirmishes, mostly between bakufu adherents and several disenfranchised families who had ties to the Heike and Fujiwara of the old order. It was futile. The Jôkyû Rebellion, named for the era in which it occurred, ended with the re-occupation of Kyôto and the forced exile of Go-Toba.

For half a century there was peace; then, during the tenure of the eighth regent, Tokimune, a letter was received from Kublai Khan, Mongol Emperor

Ashikaga Takauji. Note the pantaloon-style *haidate*. A modern reproduction of a contemporary portrait is now preserved in a Kyôto family collection.

of China, demanding tribute from the 'King of Japan', thus putting the Japanese emperor in an inferior position by using a lesser title. It was fortunate that the government faced with this threat was a military one and not the old Fujiwara-controlled court aristocracy. The reply from the shikken was a firm refusal.

The Mongol Invasions

In 1274 the Mongol armada from China, 800 ships and 30,000 men strong, arrived off the Japanese coast. The first islands on the way to Kyûshû were soon overrun. The Japanese defenders were shocked at the foreign style of fighting: warfare in Japan was highly ritualised and purely an affair between bushi, but the Mongols and their Korean conscripts conducted whole-scale massacres. Samurai were trained in individual combat, men of similar rank calling out challenges and engaging each other, whereas this foreign horde fought in huge massed formations with wholly different tactics. Frantic requests for help were sent to Kamakura.

The Mongols soon reached Kyûshû, southernmost of the four main islands, and forced the

This is a *tachi* of the Kamakura Period. It differs from the later *katana* in that the *tachi* was designed to be suspended from the *obi* edge down while the *katana* was designed to be thrust through the *obi* edge up. (Tôkyô National Museum)

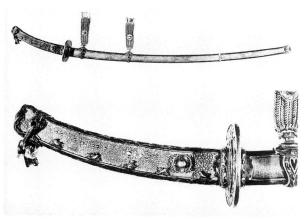

defenders to entrench. They were surprised, however, at the desperate strength of the resistance; and, having used up much of their provisions and matériel in what they had expected to be quick shock-attacks, were in serious need of resupply. The Mongol ships were pulling out of Hakata harbour in search of a safe port (fearing night-time raids while in enemy territory) when the rains began. Like an answer to a prayer, a huge typhoon hit the ships hard; and the reinforcements requested by the bakufu never had to engage the enemy. Several thousands died as their ships foundered, struck one another, or ran aground, leaving the continental soldiers as easy pickings for the samurai on shore. The few ships that were able limped back to Korea, where records show that over 13,000 men had lost their lives during the attempted invasion.

This Kamakura period *dô-maru* is in the Tôkyô National Museum collection. Note that the *shikoro* is so wide that there is almost no hang at all.

This *kabuto* is fairly typical of those of the Nanboku-chô Era. The triple-horn crest is called *mittsu-kuwagata*. (Kôzan-dô)

Expecting a second assault, the government in Kamakura constructed a huge defensive wall in Hakata Bay, the best and most likely landing site in the area. Their suspicions were confirmed when, in 1281, the second attack came. Conveniently enough, it was aimed at Hakata.

This second assault was much larger than the first: over 4,000 ships and 200,000 men were involved. Fortunately for Japan, the attack was split into two parts and the over-anxious commander of the smaller, southern fleet sailed about a month early. Again, however, the attackers were amazed at the determination of the defending samurai. So fierce was the resistance that for days, even though the ships lay in the harbours, they were unable to land their troops. The ships were small, and it was the middle of the summer. Disease and food shortages plagued the enemy. The Japanese were playing a desperate waiting game which they had no way of winning.

When the Mongols' large northern fleet arrived

at the rendezvous, however, the defending samurai knew that they could not hold off the enemy much longer. On 15 August the retired emperor's prayer for divine intervention was presented at the Ise Grand Shrine to his ancestor, the Sun goddess Amaterasu-O-mikami. That evening, a miracle occurred. The skies grew dark, and the wind began to blow. Ships were dashed against the rocks, splintered and fell apart. This was the true *kamikaze*, the spirit wind. Once again the weather had turned the invaders away; at least two-thirds of the Mongol force lost their lives.

The Khan wanted to raise a third assault, larger still, but it never materialised, probably due to resistance to the expense involved. If so, the Great Khan was not the only one feeling the financial burdens of the two invasions. The Hôjô government was nearly bankrupted in trying to reward the samurai who fought, and to pay the temples and shrines which had prayed for the victories. They

were finding that it was expensive and difficult to give rewards after a victorious campaign which had produced no new territories nor filled any coffers. There was also the considerable expense involved in the simple upkeep of the military garrisons and their fortifications. When Tokimune died in 1284, the bakufu was seriously weakened. Strong leaders were needed to fill the place of the powerful shikken; but none emerged.

War of the Northern and Southern Courts

In 1318 a new emperor by the name of Go-Daigo came to the throne. Go-Daigo looked at the severely weakened bakufu and the uninvolved, inactive shikken and decided to follow the footsteps of his ancestor Go-Toba in attempting to depose the regent and destroy the system which sustained him. He laid his plans carefully: remembering that Go-Toba had not had the support of the monks on Mt. Hiei, he even installed a son as head abbot of Enryaku-ji so as to have their sôhei on his side. Also

These are but a few of the more common forms of arrowheads employed throughout the history of samurai archery. A Heike archer or one of Ieyasu's would recognise any of these. There were also many pierced-work examples; and arrowheads designed to produce a whistling noise. (Tôkyô National Museum)

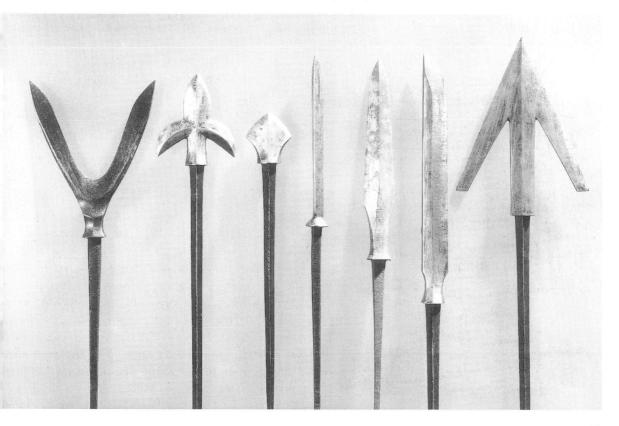

supporting him was Kusunoki Masashige, one of the great names in Japanese military annals.

In 1331 Go-Daigo fled Kyôto with the Imperial regalia, causing a bakufu assault on Enryaku-ji on Mt. Hiei. The abbot retreated to Masashige's fortress in Kawachi, where the entire Loyalist army—all 500 of them—waited for the bakufu attack. The fortress was lightly defended, so Masashige prepared an ambush by splitting his forces, half inside and half hidden in the mountains around the palisades.

Archers within took a heavy toll of the first assaults on the walls; and while they were resting, the attackers were set upon by the waiting troops hidden outside. The siege went poorly for the Loyalists, however, and Masashige was forced to resort to subterfuge. He ordered a huge funeral pyre built for the slain, and under the cover of night the remaining defenders slipped out of the fortress in ones and twos. A single samurai remained to tell the bakufu troops who entered the fortress the next day of the mass suicide of the night before, pointing to the flaming pyre deep with bodies.

The bakufu generals believed the story. Masashige retook the fortress shortly thereafter, but was subsequently forced to abandon it again, narrowly escaping once more. Now operating out of the naturally fortified Chihaya, Masashige called for assistance. The Loyalist movement grew with each day, as bakufu control slipped. Masashige became bolder, his plans more subtle and daring; he even was able to trick the enemy into thinking that they had suborned some of his men, and when they prepared to enter the 'open' gate, Masashige attacked. In their haste to retreat the bakufu force were engaged by their own comrades, mistakenly taking them for a raiding party of Loyalists from Chihaya.

This well-preserved *haramaki* is classic Kamakura Era style. Note that it was not designed to be worn with *sode*, marking it, at this period, as a retainer's armour. (Tôkyô National Museum)

Rear view of the same. The *se-ita*, or back plate, which covered the opening left by the join, is clearly visible. Some called it a 'coward's plate', implying that no one brave would need one, as the enemy would never even see his back.

The bakufu decided to end the Loyalist cause another way, by eliminating Go-Daigo: Ashikaga Takauji, who had fought Masashige at Kawachi, was sent to take the emperor prisoner. But Takauji changed sides, and in the emperor's name took Kyôto. Soon afterwards another veteran bakufu commander, Nitta Yoshisada, struck at Kamakura itself, proclaiming himself an emperor's man. On 5 July 1333 the bakufu and the Hôjô Shikken fell.

Go-Daigo, now the sole ruler, was faced by a well-armed and well-trained group of powerful and jealous men expecting their reward. One of the attempts he made to curb the power of the samurai was to appoint his own son, Prince Morinaga, shôgun. He made several other mistakes as well, often slighting the very group which had put him in power.

Takauji in particular felt that he had been given too small a reward; so when he was sent to Kamakura to quell an attempt to revitalise the bakufu, he joined the Hôjô pretender and declared war on the Loyalist cause, setting himself up as commander of Kamakura. Even without the title of shôgun, his intention was clear: he meant to set up his own bakufu.

Two Courts

The response was swift: the Loyalists rallied and forced Takauji first from Kamakura and then gradually further south. Takauji was forced back until he had to flee to Kyûshû; but after a spectacular victory against Loyalist forces there in April 1336 he was again on Honshû, the mainland. This time he had a huge army of supporters who had taken up his cause in Kyûshû.

Masashige rushed to lend assistance and reinforcements to Nitta Yoshisada, commander of the Loyalist troops. Go-Daigo ordered an attack. Masashige begged the emperor to retreat to Enryaku-ji, allowing Takauji to take the capital; the sôhei and samurai could then fall on the city and cut off any Ashikaga retreat. It was a virtually foolproof plan, and undoubtedly would have succeeded. But the emperor was not a military man and could not see the value of this tactical retreat. Military men fight, so he wanted a battle. Masashige knew it was useless, but went in to battle at the emperor's command.

On 5 July 1336 the forces of the Loyalists under

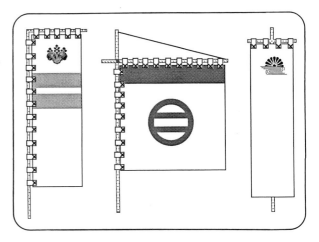

These three standards represent the most typical forms of Japanese battleflags. When large enough to be considered standards, they are called *uma-jirushi*, literally 'horse signs'.

Nitta Yoshisada and Kusonoki Masashige met the combined land and sea Ashikaga forces at Minatogawa. It was a valiant fight, but from the outset it was a lost cause. Masashige, sorely wounded and beset on all sides, committed suicide; Yoshisada was forced to retreat. Takauji entered Kyôto, and in 1337 set up an Imperial prince as the new emperor. It was not legitimate, however, as Emperor Go-Daigo still had the regalia: without it, there could be no true new emperor.

This led to a schism lasting over 50 years during which there were two emperors, two courts, and even two separate sets of era-names proclaimed by the emperors. The legitimate line of Go-Daigo, the Southern Court, was based in Yoshino in southern Nara. The new line in Kyôto, the Northern Court, was supported by and in return supported the new Ashikaga Bakufu.

In 1347 Kusonoki Masatsura, son of the late Masashige, took command of the Loyalists supporting Go-Murakami, the new Southern Emperor, Go-Daigo having died in 1339. The last remnants of the Kusonoki clan were obliterated in battle the next spring.

For the remainder of the *Nanboku-chô*—the Northern-Southern Court era—very little happened. Both courts made demands on clans, splitting many into factions as families tried to ensure that none of their interests suffered. They frequently transferred allegiance; the old order of unswerving loyalty and dedication was all but gone.

On 16 December 1392, the Southern Court

recognised the futility of their position and gave in to the inevitable. The age of rival emperors was over. The present Emperor of Japan is descended from the Northern Court.

The Muromachi Period

The Ashikaga Bakufu

Ashikaga Takauji started his government by bringing the bakufu back to Kyôto, and establishing it in the Muromachi district; this is what gives the period in Japanese history from 1338 to 1573 its name. It is also called the Ashikaga Era, for they were the undeniable rulers. Towards the end, however, their 'rule' was in name only; in truth, no one ruled.

Although the Ashikaga were descended from the Minamoto (this had become a requirement for the title of shôgun), they had little real power of their own at first. Only a small percentage of land was under direct Ashikaga family control, although they enjoyed several beneficial alliances and vassalages. This meant that they were not inherently wealthy or powerful. Ashikaga Takauji had been lucky.

Once the city had been reinstated as the capital, Kyôto enjoyed great prosperity, and many great

This woodcut shows a typical *hara-ate* from the Muromachi Era. (Honchô Gunkikô)

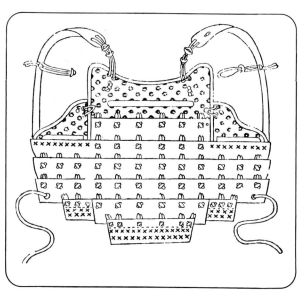

bushi families built estates there for the first time. This led to a distinct fusion of the two major powers in the land: the court nobility, which formed the civil aristocracy, and the military nobility, which formed the military government. The shôgun's palace was even built opposite that of the emperor—which it dwarfed in size.

In the late 14th century a new class of samurai aristocracy, the *shugo*, emerged. Shugo had been military governors under the Kamakura bakufu, but the office survived and even thrived under that of the Muromachi shôgunate. The shugo were made to live in Kyôto (or Kamakura if they were from the east). These shugo could be considered early *daimyô* (a later term), as both were lords of their land; the shugo, however, were more closely tied to the bakufu in the earlier years. Certainly by the end of the Muromachi Era they would all have been replaced by daimyô, with little attention paid to shôgunal authority as it waned.

It was the third Ashikaga shôgun, Yoshimitsu, who finally achieved the reunification of the Imperial court. He was an accomplished warrior and statesman, as well as a man of great culture, who could be compared favourably with any of the princes or doges in Italy as a patron of the arts—a true 'Renaissance man'. He retired from the shôgunate in 1395 when only 36, to live in the palatial retreat he built for himself in the mountains north of Kyôto. The palace's most famous hall is the 'Golden Pavilion', the Kinkakuji. Under a roof clad in gold leaf, each of the three storeys is in a distinctly different architectural style which manages to form an aesthetically pleasant synthesis. This fitted shôgun Yoshimitsu's lifestyle perfectly: warrior, artisan and statesman.

Gekokujô and the Onin War

Unfortunately, life under the Ashikaga was not always peaceful. For the first time a new force in Japan took up the sword—the peasants. Several times between 1428 and 1461, thousands of peasants in bands called *ikki* stormed into the capital. Originally they were mutual defence groups, not unlike the early sôhei. One of their main grievances was the financial burden imposed by a series of edicts. Striking out at money-lenders and others of that ilk, they burned and looted indiscriminately.

These militant peasants made a good source of arrow-fodder for the *shugo-daimyô*, who could always use more men, and who readily took them in. The peasants entered the armies at the lowest rank and were called *ashigaru* ('light feet'). They were cheap to outfit, as armour and weapons were everywhere—battlefield scavenging was a common method of acquiring or up-grading one's own equipment. The increasing size of an armed and militarily trained lower class was setting the stage for what came to be called *gekokujô*: the low overcoming the high. It was a dangerous time to be weak.

One of Japan's most devastating internal wars only affected Kyôto, but it nearly destroyed the city, and left neither side in a position to be declared victorious. It is difficult to point to any single cause of the war, but two powerful families, related by marriage, were at the heart of it.

The Yamana and the Hosokawa were in opposition to each other, but it is unclear what actually started the dispute between Hosokawa Katsumoto and his father-in-law, Yamana Sôzen, two magnates of very different character. Katsumoto, suave and cultured, was a valued counsellor to the shôgun; while Sôzen was famed for his excessive ambition, bad temper and frequent lapses of good manners. When Shôgun Yoshimasa (1443–74) attempted to resign (unlike his grandfather, he only wanted to relax and enjoy life—government bored him), there was a succession dispute between his younger brother; his deputy to whom he had promised the office; and his infant son, for whom his wife was scheming. The two enemies found themselves backing rival claimants, Sôzen the son and Katsumoto the brother. The two families had in the past been on opposite sides of familial succession disputes, but this time the dispute was for the control of Japan itself.

The first battle of the Onin War (named, like most Japanese conflicts, after the era in which it began) was fought in 1467, when Hosokawa troops attacked the mansion of a Yamana general which faced the shôgunal palace. Again, fire and looting began in the capital. The guard at the Imperial Palace was even increased, something hardly conceivable as necessary. Sure enough, Sôzen tried in 1467 to conduct a raid on the Imperial Palace, but, having heard of the plan, Katsumoto was able

This *haramaki-dô* is made of the older, wider form of scales. It is typical of the armour worn by more wealthy samurai in the Sengoku Period. The *kabuto* is a variation on the *Ichi-no-Tani* form, and the lacing is *murasaki susogo* (see Plate B). (Kôzan-dô)

to spirit the emperor and the retired emperor to the security of the bakufu headquarters.

Much of northern Kyôto was destroyed over the next few months. One battle produced so many bodies that after eight cartloads of heads had been counted, the rest were just thrown into ditches. The two sides attacked and retreated back and forth across the same land until opposing trenches were dug right across the main street of the ancient capital. Hosokawa was able to convince the shôgun to declare Yamana a rebel—possibly because the shôgun's palace was in the section of the city he controlled. Yamana, however, controlled all the exits. For months the routine of trench warfare held sway in Kyôto.

What was Shôgun Yoshimasa doing? While the war raged in the city, he occupied himself in

Ashikaga Yoshimitsu's famed Golden Pavilion, the site of many a poetry reading and moon-viewing party. It is now part of a Buddhist temple.

Warfare in Muromachi and Momoyama Japan

building a retreat along the lines of his grandfather's Golden Pavilion; his was to be covered with silver foil—the Silver Pavilion. To his chagrin, there was not enough money in the coffers to finish it, so the silver was never applied; to this day the walls are black, a fitting comment in itself. Here, as society crumbled around him, Yoshimasa continued to pursue his arts—completely oblivious to the ruin he himself had played such a vital rôle in creating.

In December 1477, after ten years of fighting, the commander of the Yamana forces (Sôzen had died of non-battle-related causes in 1473) put Kyôto to the torch and retreated. Although the Onin War was over, many of the ashigaru and other low conscripts stayed to loot, drink, and fight it out in the streets among themselves. It was months before rebuilding could start in Kyoto.

One of the results of the Onin War was that the Ashikaga bakufu was mortally weakened. The following Ashikaga shôgun were virtually puppets of the Hosokawa family.

Defence

Castles, which had never really played a part in Japanese military tradition, came into their own in the later Muromachi Era. Even the Heike and Genji had had what were called castles, but these were more comparable to the traditional image of American frontier forts, consisting of simple pallisaded walls and a few watchtowers. This was probably the same type of construction used in Kawachi and Chihaya.

Japanese military tradition had always stressed combat, and glorified in the personal contact between heroes. The ancient Western tradition of prolonged siege (as in the *Iliad*) was alien to them. It was not until the time of Kusunoki Masashige that prolonged sieges were seriously conducted. Even then, however, the true battles were initiated by sallies from the fortress or direct frontal attacks.

This is one of the most famous armours still existing in Japan: the *Tatenashi Yoroi*, an heirloom of the Takeda clan. The lacing is *kozakura-gawa-odoshi*. It is not clear when it was first made, but an armour with the same name is mentioned as one of the eight heirloom-armours of the Minamoto, and the Takeda were Minamoto descendants. It was worn by Shingen, at least, and his father. (Kanda Jinja)

A samurai wearing a *kawatsuzumi-haramaki* from around the period of the Nanboku-chô war—see Plate D. (From a contemporary illustration.)

There were attempts to overrun the defences, but nothing resembling siege engines. Had the bakufu employed battering rams or catapults, the Nanboku war would have ended quite soon. Japan, however, had none of these alien engines.

True castles, recognisable as such, started to appear in the middle of the 16th century—about the same time as the arrival of the first Portuguese and the first firearms. What effect one may have had on the other is an interesting, if academic, question. We are told, however, that the great stronghold of Oda Nobunaga, Azuchi Castle, was built with the help of a Portuguese designer.

The graceful curving lines that distinguish the foundation walls of Japanese castles served a purpose: they made them difficult to climb. This was a legacy from the earlier walled fortresses. The main donjon itself was also different in function to its Western counterpart: in the West, the donjon was the home of the lord and his family, but in Japan it was more of a military command centre. Only late in the period did some live therein—most lived in palaces built within the walls.

It is unfortunate that most of the older castles were destroyed over the years. Many were lost when the Tokugawa bakufu limited the number of castle holdings to reduce possible enemy defences. The older, less useful ones were the first to go. Many were also lost to earthquake or fires, or fell victim to attack; as recently as the Second World War many were bombed flat as incidental targets of the US Army Air Corps. Most of the famous castles in Japan today are modern ferro-concrete replicas of the originals and house museums. Fortunately for architects and historians, Japan is experiencing something of a boom in castle reconstruction; in the last few years quite a few castles have been completely or partially rebuilt.

There were three principal forms of castle: the mountain castle, the hill castle, and the plain castle. All had their strengths and weaknesses. A mountain castle would be very easy to defend, but was less than convenient to live in. A plain castle, on the open flatlands, would be easier to live in, but less easy to defend. A hill castle, built on a hill or rise in the middle of an open field, was probably the best of both worlds; defensible while not inhospitable.

Offence

Dating back to the Genpei War, fighting was primarily conducted among equals: peasant fought peasant while the commanders and officers shouted challenges and often engaged in highly ritualised single combat.

Ancient Chinese military classics such as Sun Tzu's *Art of War* were read by the samurai as far back as the 900s. Yoshitsune studied them, as did the Taira. Using his own considerable gifts and his studies of the Chinese masters, Kusunoki Masashige

A *dô-maru* of the early 15th century, from a woodblock print in the Honchô Gunkikô of Arai Hakuseki. (Author's collection)

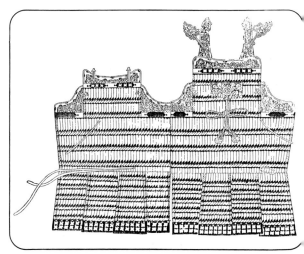

changed the face of war. Harrying the enemy, using deception and confusing them, he is considered to have been the first true *ninja* (spy) for the ways in which he operated.

Often, daimyô did not lead in battle themselves, relegating the actual field command of troops to vassal daimyô and sub-generals. This was not cowardice, however. They did go to war: they usually sited themselves in a rear position serving as a command centre. Around them would be a personal guard, and the higher-ranked retainers. These were called *hatamoto*, a word implying their position below the lord's banners. At first, all daimyô had hatamoto. Under the Tokugawa bakufu, however, only certain direct retainers of the Tokugawa were eligible for this title; it became hereditary, and ceased to refer to select loyal retainers of regular daimyô.

There were other changes in armies as the years passed. With the advent of firearms, ranks of musketeers were added to the traditional rows of pikemen, archers, and other warriors. There were a few changes in tactics to accommodate the new weapons.

The End of Muromachi Japan

One classic example of the principle of *gekokujô* is Hôjô Sôun (no relation to the long extinct shikken family of the Minamoto bakufu). He was a minor samurai who, by conquering a declared rebel ruler of Izu in 1491, was rewarded with control of the province. He changed his name to the more prestigious Hôjô and managed, by artifice or combat, to expand his clan's rule into neighbouring domains and territories. When he died his sons continued the tradition. For his origins and accomplishments, Hôjô Sôun is considered by most Japanese historians to have been the first *sengoku daimyô*; he was certainly not the last.

The *sengoku jidai*, or warring states period, was marked by many such meteoric rises—and falls. Ancient and powerful families would weaken or be supplanted, some by their own vassals; others would simply cease to be. Others, like the clan of Hôjô

Sôun would come from virtually nowhere. One of the things which contributed to the ease with which wars could be fought and won was the introduction to Japan in 1542 of a new type of weapon: the matchlock arquebus.

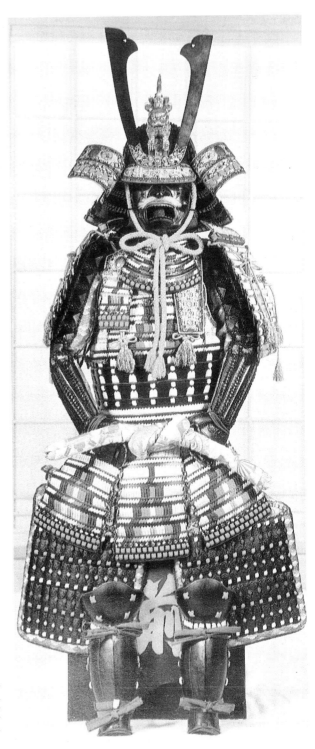

This Sengoku armour bears the unusual name *ebi-dô*, or 'shrimp cuirass'. The torso of the two-piece cuirass is laced in *sugake* while the *muneage* is laced in *kebiki*. The pattern here is *omodaka-odoshi*, using white as a base, then blue and finally red. The addition of the *sendan* and *kyubi no ita* mark this armour as Edo Period style. (Kôzan-dô)

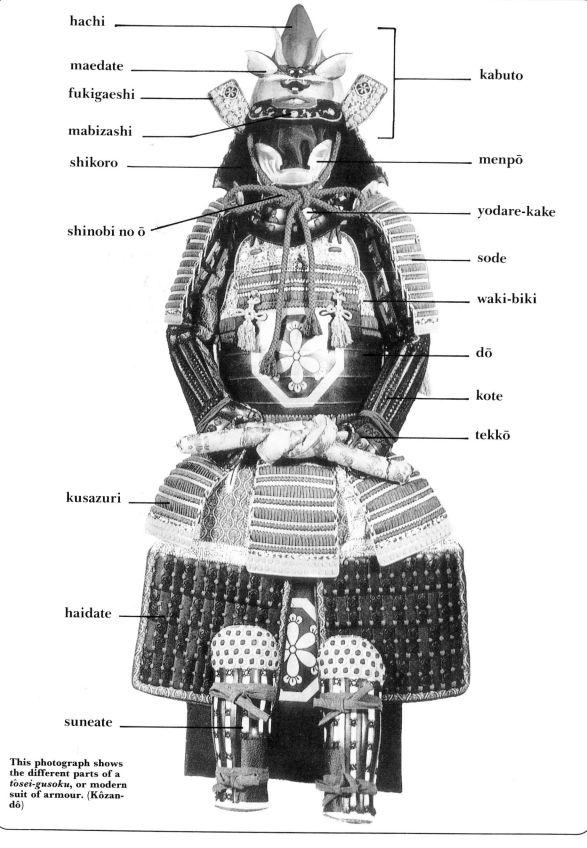

hachi

maedate

fukigaeshi

mabizashi

shikoro

shinobi no ō

kusazuri

haidate

suneate

kabuto

menpō

yodare-kake

sode

waki-biki

dō

kote

tekkō

This photograph shows the different parts of a *tôsei-gusoku*, or modern suit of armour. (Kôzan-dô)

European Influences

It seems that Kyûshû was destined to be Japan's doorstep. Whenever a foreign power wished to enter the country, they always seem to have gone through Kyûshû. The original Japanese inhabitants are believed to have entered the archipelago from Korea via Kyûshû. When the Chinese first came bringing trade and their written characters, they came through Kyûshû. When the Mongols attacked in 1274 and again in 1281, they attacked Kyûshû. Even as late as the Second World War the US attacked Kyûshû's neighbouring islands and the first planned mainland landing would have been in Kyûshû itself.

When the Mongols tried to invade, Japan had been saved by a storm that scattered and sank the invading ships. In 1542, it was a storm which brought the outsiders. In that year Fernando Mendez Pinto and two companions boarded an outward-bound Chinese ship in the Portuguese colony of Macao. A storm carried the ship off course, and it came to harbour in a port of Tanegashima, a small Kyûshû island. Tanegashima Tokitaka, governor of the island, was very impressed by the strange weapons the three Portuguese carried. He arranged to have them studied and reproduced.

Simple matchlocks, they were soon being made in increasing numbers, and more and more daimyô began to equip their armies with them. They were

Sengoku ashigaru armour was plain and protective. Often, a *mon* would be painted on the chest as a sort of uniform device. The *jingasa* form is quite common. Often, ashigaru would cook their dinner in their *jingasa*, suspending them over a fire. (Kôzan-dô)

called *teppô*, or *tanegashima*, after the island. (It is an interesting historical oddity that today the island of Tanegashima is where Japan launches her rockets and satellites.) Many ancient and aristocratic families despised the weapon as unfitting for samurai but, not surprisingly, they soon either changed their opinions or were crushed by others less idealistic.

The foreigners did not only bring guns, however. They also brought the Catholic Church, a force which would figure in future political struggles. It would sometimes be the manipulator, playing daimyô against daimyô, and sometimes the victim, caught between warring clans and rival magnates. Nobunaga would favour the Europeans with trade and audiences; and Hideyoshi would alternately favour and revile them. By the 1570s many major

Half-armoured sleeves, *han-gote*, were not very common. This well-preserved pair are of a style called *tsubo-* (tube) *gote*, because they enclosed the arm like a solid tube. Those made of splints were called *shino-gote*. *Suneate* are likewise so classified. (Private collection, Tôkyô)

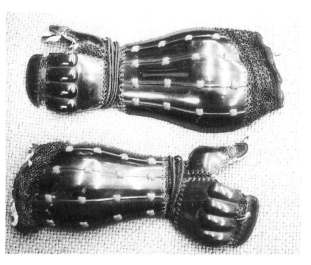

There is something about the plainness of this rust-colour-lacquered armour with its pale green lacing that sums up the entire style of 16th century armour. It is not an ornate suit, but it has a definite appeal. The style is a *tachi-dô*, a two-plate *kebiki*-laced cuirass of scale; in this case, *kiritsuke-zane*. (Kôzan-dô)

cities had cathedrals, and there were over 15,000 Christian Japanese living in central Japan alone. One high official of the Church, visiting Japan in 1582, estimated that in all of Japan there were some 150,000 adherents of the Faith.

The Last Shôgun

Descended from the Minamoto were the Imagawa, one of the older, more respected clans. They were related to the Ashikaga as well, so it was hardly surprising that they shared similar tastes and a similar lifestyle. Sumpu, their capital, was the site of lavish poetry contests and ceremonies like those seen elsewhere only in Kyôto. They even adopted the courtly affectation of whitening the skin, blackening their teeth, and painting fake eyebrows high on their foreheads, something most of the neighbouring war-lords considered decadent.

The simple truth, however, was that they were not as soft as most thought; they were very skilled in battle tactics and manoeuvre and they had the advantages of a productive, well-situated seat of power. Curiously enough, despite these strengths, they were more interested in leading the life of aesthetes. It is possible that they had allowed themselves to be lulled into a false sense of security—their neighbours were more belligerent.

In 1560 Imagawa Yoshimoto prepared to march on Kyôto to set himself up as puppet-master to a weak Ashikaga shôgun, beginning with an invasion of the domain of a neighbouring daimyô, Oda Nobunaga. Oda was one of the classic *gekokujô-daimyô*. His family was not powerful or wealthy, and his lands were not full of gold like the Takeda, or of rice like the Imagawa. His clan had risen from being weak and powerless to mildly threatening. The Imagawa were not ones to waste time, so they chose to deal with Nobunaga before he became too powerful.

One of the vassal houses of the Imagawa was that of the Tokugawa, the lord of which was 19-year-old Ieyasu (then named Matsudaira Motoyasu), who came with Yoshimoto to command one wing of the attack against Oda. Ieyasu scored an initial victory and took several fortresses guarding Oda's frontier. While the Imagawa main force rested in the valley at Okehazama, Nobunaga, in a desperate attack during a thundershower, swept down on Yoshimoto's army.

Nobunaga was outnumbered 25,000 to 2,000—better than 12 to one—yet within 15 minutes Yoshimoto was dead and the Imagawa defeated. It was an astonishing victory, which made the 26-year-old Nobunaga's reputation. Freed from his allegiance to Yoshimoto, Ieyasu even went so far as to put his support behind Nobunaga, the man who had killed his liege lord.

Several neighbouring provinces soon fell to Nobunaga, who now used Gifu, formerly an enemy stronghold, as his capital. Nobunaga had reached a plateau: he had secured his position by arranging judicious marriages between his relatives and local war-lords, but there was very little more he could accomplish without (as one of his lieutenants, Hideyoshi, said) 'a name'. In 1568, in the person of Ashikaga Yoshiaki, destiny paid a call on Nobunaga.

Yoshiaki was the rightful heir to the shôgunate; after his father's assassination, a puppet of the assassins had been set up as shôgun. Yoshiaki appealed for help, and Nobunaga responded. They entered Kyôto in November 1568, and Yoshiaki was installed as the 15th Ashikaga shôgun. He would also be the last.

With official license from the bakufu, Nobunaga set out to conquer all of Japan. Recalcitrant daimyô were branded as traitors and crushed. The co-operation between the shôgun and his patron (for such was the true situation) grew strained, and in 1573 Yoshiaki made the mistake of lashing out at Nobunaga. Nobunaga had submitted to him a list of 17 reforms which he felt the bakufu needed. One of them was that the shôgun should refrain from involvement in politics. Yoshiaki's answer was to send a message to Takeda Shingen in his home province of Kai requesting help in eliminating Oda Nobunaga. Nobunaga's response was swift; he seized the shôgun and imprisoned him, and went to make war on Takeda Shingen, to whose son his own daughter was betrothed. Such was the Sengoku Era.

Sengoku Japan

Shingen was one of the most successful daimyô of the era. His policies, both for the government of his fief and in dealings with other daimyô, were models that few could hope to match. Shingen was one of the few of his class to maintain a standing army without destroying the economy or killing agricultural output. One of the reasons for his success was the fact that he was sitting on one of Japan's most productive gold mines. He was, even by modern standards, incredibly wealthy. He did not hoard his money, however; he spent it wisely. He was able to build Kai, his mountainous province (modern Yamanashi Prefecture), into one of the most prosperous daimyates in the nation.

The Battles of Kawanakajima
Among the most distinctive events of this turbulent period was the rivalry between Takeda Shingen and Uesugi Kenshin. These two great men had a great deal in common. They were born within nine years of each other, they had both taken the tonsure, both had reached a very high rank in their respective Buddhist sects, and both were descended from great families (Kenshin from the Fujiwara,

This is a part-*okegawa*- and part-*kebiki*-laced fake-scale armour. This combination is classic Sengoku. The tall helmet crest bears the slogan *Namu Amida Butsu*, 'Hail to Amida Buddha!' (Kôzan-dô)

Shingen from the Minamoto). Both were also consummate tacticians and military commanders.

They are most famous for their long conflict at Kawanakajima. In the summers of 1553, 1554, 1555, 1556, 1557 and 1563, their two armies met in the same place. Nothing was ever decided as their battles were little more than stylised manoeuvres, so neither side won any major victory. Despite this, the battles between Shingen and Kenshin have become famous. One incident in particular stands out. Shingen was sitting, as was his wont, behind the lines waiting for word about a skirmish, when a few horses galloped up. Shingen's defenders were not suspecting a raiding party from the Uesugi lines, let alone one led personally by Kenshin. Before they could respond, Kenshin rode up to Shingen and struck at him with his sword. Shingen deflected the attack with his iron war-fan. Within minutes, the Takeda had rallied and were able to drive Kenshin off. Shingen had never drawn his sword, nor even stood up.

On Yoshiaki's behalf, or perhaps on his own, Shingen made good his promise to strike Nobunaga down. In 1573 he was engaged in an assault on one of Ieyasu's castles (Tokugawa Ieyasu had become one of Nobunaga's most highly valued commanders) when he was struck by a musket ball and died. The wound was initially not thought to have been severe, but as many histories say he was taken ill and died, the truth may well be that it became infected. Nobunaga, involved elsewhere at the time with religious rioters, rejoiced.

Ikkô-ikki

The old ikki had taken a new and belligerent form (probably provoked by the arrival of Christian missionaries whom they regarded as rivals to Buddhism), and a band called the *Ikkô-ikki* had been causing considerable trouble to Nobunaga. They were essentially a composite of the ikki and sôhei, and fiercely tied to the Jôdô ('pure land') sect. Few European crusaders would have been able to match their burning religious fervour, combined with their desire to destroy those who opposed them. As early as 1486 they had been involved in military conflicts, when they took control of the entire Kaga province. Their headquarters was the Higashi Hongan-ji in Osaka, a huge temple/monastery-cum-fortress.

They were one of Nobunaga's targets. Another was the community of monks on Mt. Hiei. It was the latter who first felt his considerable wrath; in 1571 Enryaku-ji was soundly crushed, a bloody lesson which sent shivers through Japan. The Christian missionaries, whom Nobunaga had been courting for their trade, were overjoyed: Nobunaga had shown such mercilessness to the 'enemies of God' that surely he would convert—and if he converted, surely Japan would have to follow.

But Nobunaga showed no sign of any intention to convert. He was too busy routing out the Ikkô-ikki next. In 1574 he built up an enclosure around defiant militants and set it on fire, killing all the defenders; some 20,000 perished in the conflagration and the shooting which followed as some tried vainly to escape.

The next year found Nobunaga and Ieyasu together fighting Katsuyori, Shingen's son. Though he had inherited the Takeda clan, he had not inherited the skills of his father. Nobunaga lined up his arquebusiers behind palisades at Nagashino and awaited the assault. His numbers were far superior

The *momonari-kabuto* was a fairly common style in the late medieval period. This one is decorated with a black sun disc. (Nagatani-dera)

to Katsuyori's and it is a wonder that Katsuyori ever chose to attack. Nobunaga arranged nearly 3,000 musketeers in three ranks to facilitate continuous fire: while one rank fired, two would be reloading. The Takeda army, charging in wave after wave, was mown down in a hail of gunfire. The fact that the gunners were ashigaru and that it was therefore ashigaru who had destroyed the élite of the Takeda army was not lost on the samurai of either side.

In 1582 Nobunaga was involved in a campaign to subdue the last few daimyô holding out in the western provinces. He was en route south bringing reinforcements to his associate Hashiba Hideyoshi when he stopped to spend the night in Honno-ji in Kyôto. One of his own generals, Akechi Mitsuhide, attacked the temple and set it on fire, and Nobunaga perished in the assault. Legend says he committed *seppuku*, but no one knows for certain how he met his death.

Another *momonari*, this one has a peculiar *shikoro* made of small square plates. This form of *shikoro* was not common, but it could be seen fairly regularly in large groups. (Hôriku-ji)

This *haramaki-dô* is a replica of one worn by Uesugi Kenshin. The mail-lined skirt under the helmet was called an under-*shikoro*; Ieyasu also had a *kabuto* fitted with one. (Kôzan-dô)

Why did Mitsuhide strike out at his lord? Many possible reasons have been advanced, but the overriding one is probably connected with Nobunaga's having allowed Mitsuhide's mother, who was hostage to a rival, to be executed. Mitsuhide was able to secure control of Kyôto, and styled himself 'shôgun'.

Hashiba Hideyoshi

Ieyasu and Hideyoshi both knew that whoever put down the traitor would be in the best position to take Nobunaga's place. Ieyasu began a dangerous and tortuous forced march towards Kyôto through brigand-haunted mountains with only a handful of men. Hideyoshi was involved in a protracted siege on Nobunaga's behalf against a very powerful and hostile daimyô. The Môri stronghold at Takamatsu Castle was situated on low-lying land. Hideyoshi had dammed a river and filled in ravines, managing to bring the water-level up to the walls of the castle and very neatly flooding the defenders. The castle's fall was imminent when the news of Nobunaga's death arrived. Hideyoshi swiftly came to terms with Môri Terumoto, who had been preparing to face disaster, and hastened to Kyôto, knowing that Ieyasu would also be heading there.

It was only 13 days after Nobunaga's assassination when Hideyoshi caught up with Mitsuhide

at Yamazaki and slew him, avenging Nobunaga's death. In the eyes of the samurai it was a victory for justice; but Hideyoshi saw it as an opportunity, and he was never one to let an opportunity go to waste. He declared Nobunaga's infant grandson, Hidenobu, the rightful heir; and became the lad's protector as leader of a council of generals acting in the child's name. His policy in allowing the council was well thought-out. There would inevitably be jealousies among its powerful members, and rival claims by Nobunaga's remaining sons would often bring matters to a halt. This would allow Hideyoshi a great deal of freedom of manoeuvre.

There were, of course, defections from the 'Nobunaga' camp, which Hideyoshi gladly put down as treasonous, leading armies against the daimyô who were disinclined to support him. This served the dual purpose of maintaining the illusion of fidelity to his late master, and adding considerably to the lands under his control. As was expected of him as the leader of these campaigns, he made awards of money and land to the daimyô and generals who helped him, building up a loyal following. In a matter of months he had become the focal point of power, and the illusion of his loyalty to Nobunaga's memory was banished once and for all.

It was probably at the battle of Shizugatake in 1583, against Shibata Katsuie, that Hideyoshi decided upon the path he would take. It was an easy victory, but it made him undisputed master, and for this reason the battle deserves a greater place in Japanese history than it holds. As master of Japan, Hideyoshi realised that he had to prove his ability to govern as well as to wage war.

Oda Nobunaga's legacy to him included a well-organised army; the memory of cruel excesses committed against enemies, and coldness towards even his friends; and, interestingly, at least the appearance of a serious intention to open Japan more widely to foreign trade. (Several of his sons had been baptised Christians—even his grandson and heir would be baptised, and christened Paul.) The dead man's plans were, however, academic: Hideyoshi was in complete command.

Hideyoshi had always shown great bravery and

Decoration of this sort, gold filigree inlay added to the lacquerwork, was common with a *hotoke-dô*. The metal plates are all a russet brown. The helmet is a shot-proof type favoured by many samurai in the late 16th century. (Kôzan-dô)

creativity in his military career; one of his earliest victories for Nobunaga had been the construction of a fortress as a base for attack against an enemy castle while under the very eyes of the defenders. It is perhaps surprising that he did not in fact come from the samurai class. He was born the son of a poor wood-cutter in an obscure village called Nakumara (literally, 'Middletown'). According to some biographers he was at one time a lowly servant of a daimyô named Matsushita, and was entrusted with some money to buy for his master an *okegawa-dô* cuirass. Instead he took the money, bought armour for himself, and then enlisted with Nobunaga.

One of Hideyoshi's achievements is comparable to the Domesday Book of William the Conqueror. Begun in 1583, this province-by-province survey of Japan eventually listed every rice field in the nation, and showed how the country's wealth was spread. It was the most elaborate land survey ever conceived in Japan, and was not finished until 1598. Three copies of the register, complete with detailed maps, were made; the emperor and Hideyoshi each got one, and the daimyô of a province got his section. From that time on, provinces were spoken of in terms of *koku*: one koku of rice was the measure which could feed a man for a year. A minimum of 10,000 koku was needed to qualify as a daimyô. One of the wealthiest *han*, or fiefs, was that of the Maeda clan, valued at over a million koku. Hideyoshi had shown that he was more than a soldier; he was also an administrator.

In 1584 Tokugawa Ieyasu re-entered the scene at Nagakute, where he gave battle against Hideyoshi. The battle was more of a waiting game, as the two armies stared at each other for days from behind hastily erected barriers. Hideyoshi prepared to sneak away and attack Ieyasu's undefended home province of Mikawa. Ieyasu had expected the move, and had already set troops in position to prevent Hideyoshi's forces from leaving. When the battle was over Ieyasu had lost 600, and Hideyoshi's losses were 2,500. They then sat down to continue the stand-off. In the end, however, Ieyasu

capitulated to Hideyoshi's rule. He realized that he was younger, and could afford to be more patient.

In 1585 the emperor bestowed upon Hideyoshi the title of kanpaku. The next year he was made chancellor, and had the name Toyotomi ('an abundance of treasures') conferred on him. He stopped using Hashiba, a name he had adopted while in Nobunaga's service, putting that period of his life forever behind him. The humble-born ashigaru was now virtual master of Japan. He tried

Save for the breastplate, this armour would scarcely be taken for anything but native style. In fact, it is typical of what was done to foreign armours received as gifts to make them appeal to samurai tastes. The helmet gives the armour away as not truly foreign produced but merely a domestically-produced copy of foreign style. While the helmet retains certain features of the cabasset, the overall lines are markedly Japanese. (Kôzan-dô)

to convince people that his family was actually Fujiwara, even adopting (with Imperial blessing) the semi-regal pawlonia crest, but no one actually believed him.

Before he could rule *all* of Japan, however, he had to put down an insurrection in Kyûshû. The powerful Shimazu clan aimed to do to Kyûshû what Hideyoshi had done to the mainland, and with the help of the Christian Arima clan had nearly succeeded. Only Otomo Yoshimune, a willing vassal to the kanpaku, stood between them and rule of the entire island. At Yoshimune's request, Hideyoshi sent armies to Kyûshû to assist in the defence against the Shimazu. At first the Shimazu were victorious, but that was before all of Hideyoshi's armies had landed. In a manner very

This is the typical battle camp formation during the mid-to late-16th century. The section marked 'archers' would also, habitually, contain arquebusiers (*teppô-tai*). The section marked 'consultants' would usually consist of high-ranking retainers and vassals.

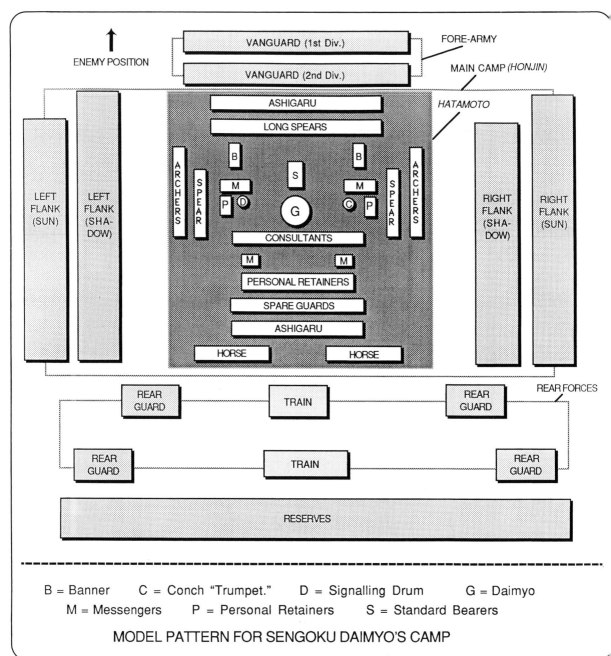

MODEL PATTERN FOR SENGOKU DAIMYO'S CAMP

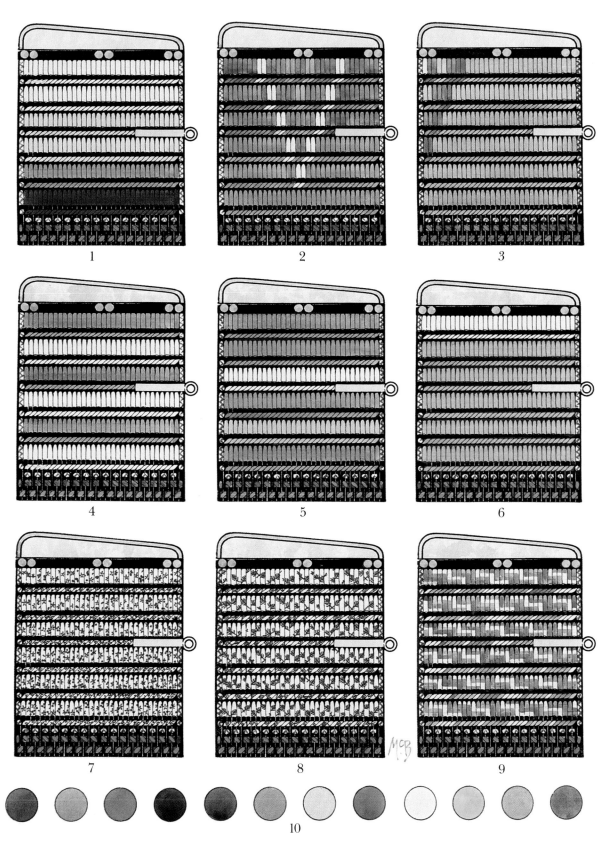

Common armour lacing styles – see commentary for details.

A

Tenko-no-Ran, AD 940
1: Taira no Masakado
2: Officer of Masakado's force
3: Retainer of Masakado's force

B

Ichi-no-Ran, 1184
1: Minamoto no Kurô Yoshitsune
2: Satô Tadanobu
3: Ise no Saburô Yoshimuri
4: Musashibô Benkei

C

D

The Mongol Invasion, 1281
1: Mounted samurai commander
2: Low-class bushi
3: Samurai
4: Sino-Mongol soldier
5: Sino-Mongol commander

Minatogawa, 1336
1: Kusunoki Masashige
2: Samurai attendant
3: Court nobleman

F

Gekokujô, c.1553
1: Samurai
2, 3, 4: Ashigaru

G

Okehazama, 1560
1: Imagawa Yoshimoto
2: Soldier of Nobunaga's force
3: Oda Nobunaga
4: Imagawa retainer

H

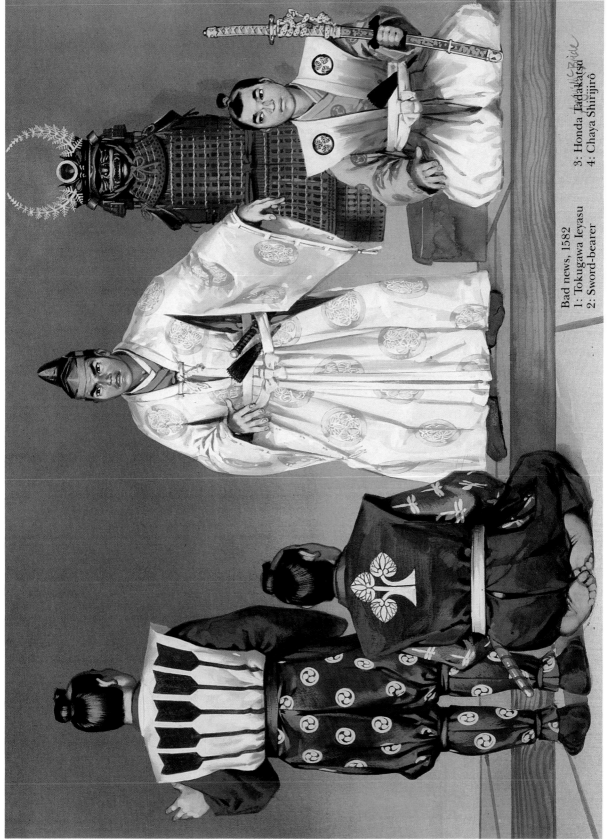

Bad news, 1582
1: Tokugawa Ieyasu
2: Sword-bearer
3: Honda Tadakatsu
4: Chaya Shirijirō

I

2

3

1

J

Sekigahara, 1600
1: Tokugawa Ieyasu
2: Honda Tadatsugu
3: Date Masamune
4: Ii Naomasa
5: Kuroda Nagamasa

K

Ashigaru, c.1600

3

2

1

L

reminiscent of Nagashino, a Shimazu force suffered its first major defeat.

One by one their 'allies' and vassals capitulated to Hideyoshi. It was a long drawn-out campaign, but in the end it was a victory for the kanpaku, who showed remarkable leniency in not putting the entire clan to the sword as Nobunaga would have done. He did, however, assign certain valuable domains to those he knew were faithful to him and would keep a watch on the Shimazu.

By the end of the campaign to subdue the Shimazu, the only clans who had yet to acknowledge Hideyoshi's suzerainty were the Hôjô in Odawara and the Date in Mutsu. In 1590, during a siege more like an extended picnic than a battle, Ieyasu took the Odawara stronghold of the Hôjô in the name of the kanpaku.

Date Masamune, so great a general that many historians have speculated that had he been born 20 years earlier he would have ruled Japan, also saw the value in submitting to Hideyoshi at about this time and did so.

The Korean Campaign

One of Hideyoshi's greatest dreams was to rule an empire. To him there was only one thing bigger than Japan, and that was China. Even as the Chinese had tried to invade Japan in the 13th century, now Japan would be the invader of China. On the way, Hideyoshi would start with Korea.

Some have pointed out that one of the reasons that Hideyoshi might have wanted to undertake this campaign was to keep his well-trained and battle-experienced samurai busy. After decades of war culminating in his conquest of Japan, he did not want to face the possibility of rebellion by any of his bored, battle-hungry vassals.

Hideyoshi's plan for attack was rather grand in scale. The invasion would be carried out in two waves. The first was seven divisions of troops which would take Korea, they were to be followed by a further three which would join them to take China itself. The vanquished Korean army would supply the further manpower required. Some 140,000 men (all but about 30,000 from Kyûshû and Shikoku) made up the first invasion force, with about 60,000 in reserve for the second wave. In 1592, the first assault force left Japan.

Hideyoshi did not go to Korea himself, and with

There were essentially two types of *hachi* (helmet bowl): *tsuji* (ribbed), and *hoshi* (star, i.e., riveted) *bachi*. With 16 plates, this is a common *tsuji kabuto*. Some master armourers produced ribbed helmets of up to 120 plates, but samurai armour historians scorned them as not battle-quality. (Kôzan-do)

For a time, near the mid-to late 16th century, *hoshi kabuto* were replaced by *tsujui* kabuto, but the former staged a very successful comeback. *Hoshi kabuto* were originally intended for a small number of plates, but this style is representative of those of the late Sengoku. Note that the 'scales' on the *shikoro* are merely cut and built up from a solid plate, a style called *kiritsuke zane*. (Kôzan-dô)

no single overall commander designated, there was considerable conflict between division commanders. The lack of rapport between the two leaders Katô Kiyomasa and the Christian daimyô Konishi, particularly, bode ill for the invaders. Had the two co-operated rather than split up in an attempt to beat each other to the capital as the armies fought their way north from Pusan to Seoul, they would have been able to take the king hostage. Instead, he was able to get away a day or two before the first division reached the royal city.

Tiger-hunting became a popular diversion for the invading samurai as they struggled north towards China. The army took P'yong-yang in 1593, the northern-most Korean fortress. It was time for the second assault force, and the attack on China, the Middle Kingdom itself.

The Korean navy, commanded by Admiral Yi Sun-Sin, entered the scene at this point. According to some sources, many of his ships were actually ironclads, and were called 'turtle-ships' partly from their iron 'shells' and partly from the fact that they were over-planked with curving boards to provide defence against boarders. By contrast, the Japanese ships were little more than barges. Using superior naval tactics and highly advanced warships, Yi was able to cut the lines of communication and harry incoming ships.

The Chinese joined the war by sending troops across the Yalu River, and the Japanese began a slow, bloody retreat to the south. Finally they were forced back to the tip of south-west Korea, where they sat for four years.

In 1597 Hideyoshi ordered a second invasion. The Chinese, however, had dug in in the north. By the end of 1598 the samurai had been forced to leave Korea. That was the year that Hideyoshi died, leaving an infant son to follow him.

The Return of the Shôgun

While Hideyoshi was busy consolidating his power after the death of Nobunaga, the patient Tokugawa Ieyasu had pulled back into his own provinces and set about strengthening his position—financially, militarily, and socially. He cultivated a few alliances, and built up his coffers. After nominally capitulating to Hideyoshi he was biding his time. His territory, centred in Edo (present-day Tôkyô), was far enough from the south that his army was spared being sent to Korea. This left him, at Hideyoshi's death, with the largest standing army in Japan, and with an annual income of 2,557,000 koku.

The Battle of Sekigahara

Hideyoshi left a council of regents to govern for and serve as guardians to his son, Hideyori, until he reached his majority. As one of the regents, Ieyasu found his greatest rival in Hideyoshi's old companion Ishida Mitsunari. Ishida, like Hideyoshi, was low-born; Ieyasu was a son of the Minamoto. The lines were being drawn.

On 21 October 1600, at the plain called

Lacing pattern of *kebiki-odoshi*. This pattern follows 13-hole *kozane*, the older fashion. Later armours would use 14-holes, and the lacing pattern was easier. Note how the rows of suspensory braid have to go between scales to reach the holes. This had the advantage of pinching on the lacing and preventing the lames from slipping.

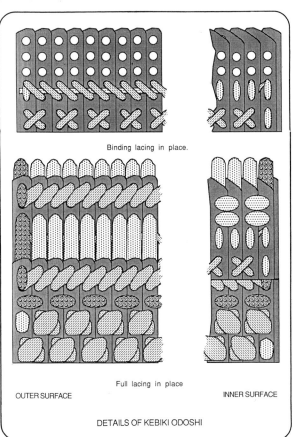

Binding lacing in place.

Full lacing in place.

OUTER SURFACE

INNER SURFACE

DETAILS OF KEBIKI ODOSHI

Arms and Armour: Heian and Kamakura Japan

The early samurai considered their primary weapon to be the bow, so the older armours reflect mounted combat thus armed. The most representative armour of the period (and of samurai in general) would be the box-like *ô-yoroi*. This consisted of a cuirass of lamellar construction with three large *kusazuri* (tassets), which left the wearer's right side exposed. This was protected by a separate, solid plate, pendant from which was the fourth kusazuri. The front of the torso was covered with a stencilled or patterned leather bib called the

Yarô-kabuto, such as this one, were one form of *kawari-kabuto*. *Yarô* implies someone from the country, and so this helmet represents the head of a rustic. It usually features bear fur over a *zunari-kabuto*. (Kôzan-dô)

Sekigahara, the battle began. Ishida Mitsunari had over 100,000 loyalist troops in the field, and Ieyasu 75,000. The weather was foggy and wet. Almost from the start it was hand-to-hand, with mass desertions from Ishida's side to Ieyasu's. In a few hours it was over, and Ieyasu was master of Japan. The single most important and decisive battle in the history of Japan had left 30,000 dead in the field. Three years later the title of shôgun was conferred on Tokugawa Minamoto no Ieyasu.

In 1615 the last remnants of the old regime were swept away in the two conflicts known as the Osaka Summer and Winter Campaigns. Hideyori, now grown up, summoned to his aid old retainers and those disaffected by the Tokugawa bakufu. Ieyasu went to put down the 'rebels,' which he did most efficiently, leaving him free to develop his new military bureaucracy. The Sengoku Era was over.

The unusual decorations on this *eboshi-nari kabuto* take the form of a pawlonia crest. The basic shape of the helmet is that of a samurai cap allowed to stand straight. It was a fairly common style, as *kawari-kabuto* go. (Tôkyô National Museum)

tsurubashiri, which was designed to allow the bowstring to pass along the chest without snagging.

As these early *yoroi* were almost without exception lacquered black, the lacing which held the scales together was the means used to lend colour to the armour. It was either dyed or patterned leather, or thick, brightly coloured silk braid, offering evidence as to the origin of the Japanese term for lacing, *odoshi-ge*; *odoshi* comes from the verb *odosu*, to intimidate, and *ge* is from the word for hair.

The *hachi* (helmet bowl) was round and heavy, often with huge, knobbed rivets. The *shikoro* (pendant nape guard) originally hung near vertical, but later would become wider and wider until it resembled nothing so much as an umbrella. Huge *fukigaeshi* ('blow backs') were attached to the front of the *shikoro* and spread out and back like wings on either side. Their original purpose seems to have been to prevent the downstroke of a sword from severing the lacing.

Kabuto (helmets) always showed a marked tendency to be back-heavy due to the weight of the *shikoro*, causing many samurai to wear their helmets

tilted forward. This habit prompted one samurai to advise a younger friend to 'lean your helmet forward but be careful that no arrow enters through the hole in your helmet'. He was referring to the *tehen*, a hole in the centre of the dome of the *hachi*. There have been many theories as to its purpose, ranging from a simple air-vent to an opening to allow the war-god Hachiman to enter and inspire the samurai to glory. It is likely, though, that the purpose was utilitarian: it occurs at the hub of the many segment-shaped plates which make up the *kabuto*, which is easier to construct without having a central point where as many as 20 (and later up to 120) layers of metal converge, so the tips were cut away and the resulting hole was decorated with a copper or gilt ring.

Commanders would often attach gilt horns called *kuwagata* to their helmets as a sign of rank. In later centuries these and similar helmet crests would be commonly worn by even the rank and file samurai.

Shoulders were protected by *sode*, which were broad, long and flat, measuring more than a foot square. Since the samurai's primary weapon was the six-foot bow used from horseback, it would have been impossible for him to use a shield and the *sode* served in its stead.

Armoured sleeves, called *kote*, were also worn

Sword guards during the medieval period (12th to 17th centuries) were usually of worked iron, such as this example from the large collection at the Tôkyô National Museum.

Starting about the 1550s, more and more finely detailed pierced work *tsuba* such as this example in the collection of the Tôkyô National Museum, were being made.

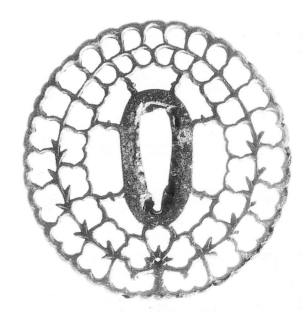

with the *ô-yoroi*. Initially only the left one was worn, and this was more to secure the bulky sleeve out of the way of the bow-string than to protect the arm. The earliest examples even seem to lack plate and mail, being little more than an (occasionally) padded bag. By the mid-13th century, samurai seem to have begun wearing a pair.

The only leg armour worn in Heian and early Kamakura Japan was the close-fitting *suneate* (shin guard). It was not until the 1300s that a need was seen for more protection on the thighs than that provided by the *kusazuri* (tassets). *Suneate* originally ended below the knees, but plates would later be added to the tops to guard the thighs of mounted warriors.

One of the earliest pieces of evidence for the existence of thigh armour is a picture of the first Ashikaga shôgun, Takauji (1305–58), who is depicted mounted, wearing a pair of *haidate*. During this period and later they were seldom worn by unmounted soldiers because they restricted movement considerably.

The armour of the common soldier was more tight-fitting and lighter than the much more costly and showy *ô-yoroi* worn by his superiors. His armour allowed a wider range of movement and was thus more suited to foot combat. Standard fighting gear for a Heian foot soldier seems to have been only a face protector and a *dô*. Those of slightly higher rank had helmets of one form or another (often acquired on the battlefield), but most had to make do with metal bands on a head cloth or a close-fitting forehead guard. They occasionally had *suneate* and *kote*. It was they who needed· the arm protection, after all.

This armour was called *dô-maru* ('torso round') as it was one piece which wrapped around the body and tied closed under the right arm. There was no *tsurubashiri* (bib), and the *kusazuri* were greater in number and reduced in bulk, thus weighing less and affording more protection. Other than this, the method of construction and general appearance was not unlike the *ô-yoroi*. Its brother was the *haramaki-dô* ('belly-wrap torso'); the two are

virtually identical, but the latter has its fastening up the back rather than under the right arm.

During the Kamakura Period, the lowest-ranked *bushi* wore the newly devolved *hara-ate* ('belly protector'), which resembled, and was no doubt based upon, the front half of the *haramaki-dô*. Of all the armours ever to have appeared in Japan, this

The emaciated torso of a Buddhist monk is reflected in the *niô-dô*. This particularly well-made example is lacquered in brick-red. The plates on the *kote* and *haidate* are variously gold and red on black lacquered mail; the effect is quite striking. The helmet, to continue the anthropomorphic illusion, is a *yarô-kabuto*. (Tôkyô National Museum)

was the simplest and cheapest. Well into the 19th century samurai would wear *hara-ate* under their court robes to give a martial air without suffering the discomfort of wearing a full suit of armour.

In fact, the samurai soon realised that the armour worn by their lessers was better in many respects than their own. Counted among the advantages of the *dô-maru* and the *haramaki* were lighter weight, greater comfort, freedom of movement, more protection, and (although this was not actually a concern to class-conscious *bushi*) cheapness.

A typical *Sendai-dô gusoku*, or suit of armour in the *Sendai-dô* style. The 'pocket' on the waist is to hold bullets. The armour comes with *sode*, which do not quite fit and so have to hang lower owing to the *ko-hire*. The helmet is a 72-plate, with a short, wide *shikoro*. (Kôzan-dô)

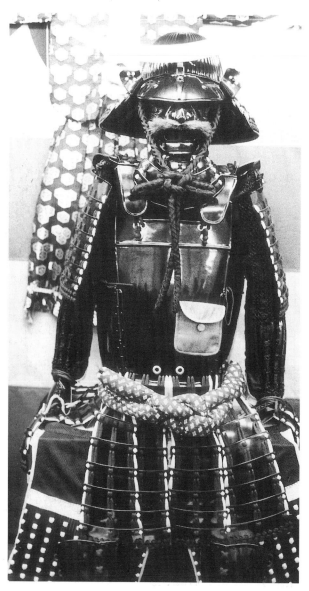

Arms and Armour: Muromachi and Momoyama Japan

By the late 14th century, even nobles were often seen wearing the *dô-maru* or *haramaki*. These noble samurai, however, retained the huge *sode*, and somehow continued to look upper-class.

The *haramaki* and *dô-maru* were commonly worn thereafter for combat, while the *ô-yoroi* was generally reserved for dress. There were, of course, many who persisted in using the great armour in battle as well as on parade, but their numbers grew fewer as the years passed. Eventually it seems that only heads of the most ancient and noble houses continued to use the *ô-yoroi* at all.

The *sode*, also a casualty of the search for comfort and convenience, shrank to a mere quarter of its old size. Makers began to curve it slightly, providing a better fit and reducing its tendency to move about.

In the 14th century the *shikoro* began to resemble an open umbrella, shallow and wide. It then began to draw in again, closer to the head and neck, as the 'warring states' period progressed.

The scales grew smaller, and more and more patterns of *odoshi-ge* came into vogue. Friend and foe vied with each other to have the most ornate and elaborate armour, to stand out more on the field of battle. The 15th and 16th centuries were among the most colourful and gaudy, and continually taxed the imaginations of the armourers.

By the Onin War, the *ô-yoroi* had been nearly completely replaced. A new armour would now be needed for the ashigaru, as the *dô-maru* and *haramaki* were expensive and time-consuming to make and repair, especially in time of war. They were no longer considered appropriate for the lower classes.

Around 1500 an armourer decided to make the *dô-maru* of solid plates rather than solidly laced board-rows of scale. He made the armour with each 'step' hinged in four places so that it could wrap about the wearer as the *dô-maru* had done, and with a clever application of saw and lacquer contrived to make the lames appear to be of true scale construction rather than a more mundane single plate. It was quickly realised that solid plates, even honeycombed as they were with holes, were more sturdy and protective than a board made up of scales measuring $2\frac{1}{2}$ in. by $\frac{5}{8}$ in. with as many as 13 holes per scale. Still, the new *Mogami-dô* (named after the region where it was developed) was at first allocated to the low-ranked troops.

Quite predictably, within 20 years the daimyô were wearing them as well. The more wealthy continued to wear armours of *hon-kozane* ('true small-scale'), however. Lesser samurai had *Mogami-dô* made using paired-strand, sparse lacing (*sugake-odoshi*) rather than the traditional full lacing (*kebiki-odoshi*).

Kebiki-odoshi had a marked tendency to weigh the wearer down when wet, was very difficult to clean, and was a snug home for vermin on extended campaigns. In addition to partly alleviating these problems, the newer sparse lacing had other advantages. With fewer holes, the plates were stronger. They were also much less expensive.

Even for nobility there was no attempt to hide the solid plate construction; most plates were plain. The reason was simple: on conventional scale armour, *sugake-odoshi* looked awful. Only on the wider style of scale called *iyô-zane* was sparse lacing ever popular.

Sode were made of solid lames en suite with the new armour, and were ever after called *Mogami-* or *tosei-* (modern) *sode*. Some were even constructed so as to be an integrated unit with the *kote*.

Soon, clamshell armours appeared with only a single hinge up the left side and the closure up the right. Many of these early armours were made of *iyô-zane*, and were called *nuinobe-dô*.

The *Mogami-dô* or *nuinobe-dô* were, by the middle of the 16th century, virtually standard for most samurai. There remained some conservatives who now preferred the *dô-maru* or *haramaki*, but these, again, were the older, more aristocratic and traditional families.

In about 1550 a revolution occurred in the world of Japanese armour when the first *okegawa-dô* ('tub-sided cuirass') made their appearance. These were clamshells, similar to the *nuinobe-dô*, but were solidy riveted, not laced; the only lace remaining was on the *kusazuri*. This armour could be made shot-proof, a necessity with the new weapon introduced by the Portuguese at about this time.

Some armour historians have speculated that beyond the protection needed from the new weapons, the *okegawa-dô* was also an adaption of the Portuguese cuirass. This is possible, as the appearance of the *okegawa-dô* followed closely the arrival of the first foreigners. Be that as it may, it would also have been the next logical step in the evolution of Japanese armour.

European armours were prized by the samurai, but as very few reached Japan replicas were often ordered from armourers. (One variety of *okegawa-dô* has a deep vertical chest ridge in imitation of the peascod cuirass.) To the cuirass they appended *kusazuri*, and to the helmet, a *shikoro*. With *sode*, *suneate*, and *kote*, the combination was striking.

More new armour designs appeared in the last half of the 16th century than ever before. Most of these were variations on, or refinements or developments of, the *okegawa-dô*.

One variation, an *okegawa-dô* which had been smoothed over by applications of lacquer and fabric leaving a rounded smooth surface, was the *hotoke-dô*

Takeda Shingen, the redoubtable war-lord of Kai. (Koyasan-ji)

One of the heavy, high-sided shot-proof helmets of the type made famous by the Haruta School. (Kôzan-dô)

Masamune himself wore a plain black *Sendai-dô* with dark blue *odoshi-ge*.

Sode were seldom worn with these modern armours, especially *Sendai-dô*. Foot combat had long eclipsed mounted warfare, and they became inconvenient and unpopular, as they restricted the range of movement necessary to wield a sword. At first they got smaller and smaller, but by the 1570s they were rarely used, according to contemporary sources. Their place was taken by small semi-circular plates or brigandine pads covering the edge of the shoulder. To be sure, armours were still equipped with *sode*, but with the little 'wings' (as these semi-circular projections over the shoulder were called), wearing *sode* had become even less convenient.

Multi-plate *kabuto* (helmets) with plates radiating out from the hub of the *tehen* continued to be the standard, but the number of plates varied from six to as many as 120 or more. The latter were, of course, rare: most considered them nothing but *tours de force* by armourers, and they were worn only by the wealthiest of daimyô who could afford such a display. More commonly, *kabuto* were of 16 or 36 plates. There was a *kabuto* of eight plates which was designed for mass-production with an eye to outfitting whole armies, but most men of rank scorned them.

The *shikoro* again curved downward from its excessively wide umbrella-like appearance at around the time of the Onin War. It was fitted closer, making head and neck movement a bit more comfortable, and even slightly easing the inconvenient back-heaviness typical with *kabuto*. For the ashigaru, however, there was only the low, conical *jingasa*.

The appearance of the simple, functional-looking three-plate *zu-nari* ('head-shaped') *kabuto* of the Hineno and Etchû schools in around 1550 opened a new era for helmet design. It became typical issue for many armies of the day, as it was cheap, quick and easy to produce, and was simple to bullet-proof. This latter feature even endeared it to daimyô and wealthier samurai, who favoured its protective qualities while disliking its commonness. To conceal the pedestrian origins of their *kabuto*, they began using lacquer, wood, and papier mâché to sculpt helmets which looked like faces, court caps, animal heads, etc. The tall court cap *kabuto* of Katô

('Buddha torso', after the smooth rounded bellies so often seen in Buddhist statuary). Most later *hotoke-dô* were made of a single plate hammered out, rather than the built up *okegawa-dô*. It was popular primarily due to the smooth surface which could readily be decorated by any number of means.

One off-shoot of the *hotoke-dô* was a *dô* embossed to represent a distended stomach and sagging breasts, ribs clearly showing; the idea was to represent the torso of a poor monk. Surprisingly, there were actually several recognised and separately-named versions of this type.

A certain form of *okegawa-dô* with vertically rather than horizontally-laminated plates, was the *Yuhinoshita*—or *Sendai-dô*. This armour was simple, plain, and very protective. It was the favoured style of Date Masamune, who equipped his whole army with them. The only distinctions of rank lay in the quality and nature of the fittings. In a historical parallel to Napoleon's favoured colonel's uniform,

Kiyomasa is one well-known example.

Kote remained for the most part unchanged. More mail would be applied, and the protective plates became smaller and greater in number. One popular style, commonly called *Kaga-gote* after the region producing the greatest numbers, was mail with an odd, gourd-shaped plate on the forearm. Sometimes these plates were hollow and hinged, and contained medicines or writing implements.

Suneate were often solid plate splints connected by strips of mail. The rising knee protectors were usually the characteristic Japanese brigandine of hexagonal plates outline-stitched and cross-laced into place with threads of contrasting colours to the facing fabric.

Haidate now completely resembled an armoured apron split up the middle. Together with the *sode*, they continued to be supplied with armour despite the fact that they were seldom worn or used in combat; both could be inconvenient when fighting on the run.

The Plates

A: Common armour lacing patterns

At some point, possibly in the early Edo Period, an attempt was made to define the colours of lacing and patterns to fit different traits and personalities, in the same way that European heralds later tried to define tinctures as representing 'nobility', 'perseverance', and 'faith', and the various heraldic charges took on new symbolic meanings which would have been lost on the original bearers of the devices. It is almost certain that there was no special meaning in the lacing used by earlier samurai, as many of them had several different suits with varied patterns and colours of lace. In this plate we see a few representative examples of the typical lacing patterns used in Japanese armour. Single-colour *odoshige* was also fairly common; it was standard with *sugake-odoshi*. Many of the patterns depicted here had alternative colours, so these are not the only choices that were available to the samurai. Often encountered in lacing are the words *ito* and

kawa (or *gawa*). They refer respectively to silk braid and leather thongs; thus, *shiro-ito-odoshi* is white silk braid, and *kuro-gawa-odoshi* is black leather thong.

A1: Susogo-odoshi

This lacing pattern is marked by the use of a single colour, graded light to dark from the top. Often the top row of lace would be white, followed by a row of

The *sode* and *kote* of this simple *okegawa-dò*, though made of solid lames, are laced in *kebiki-odoshi* in alternating blue and white rows. (Kôzan-dô)

yellow, then the grading would begin; only occasionally would the grading start from the top. Most common is *murasaki-susogo* (see Plate C) followed by *kurenai-susogo* (pictured here), *kon susogo*, *moegi-susogo*, and so on. A reverse lacing (darkest on the top, with the white row on the bottom) is called *nioi-odoshi*; this became popular during the Genpei War.

A2: Omodaka-odoshi

The name is taken from a plant, the leaf of which this pattern is said to resemble. It is one of the oldest patterns, judging from battle scrolls, although there are only a few surviving old armours laced with *omodaka-odoshi*. An older version is *saga-* (inverted) *omodaka-odoshi*. There does not seem to have been any single order for the colours, but if the foundation (here it is *moegi*) is dark, the first pyramid would be white.

A3: Tsumadori-odoshi

This is in a way similar to *omodaka* with only a single corner showing. The foundation lace would set the name: *murasaki-ito-tsumadori*, *shiro-ito-tsumadori*, and so on. This one is *asagi-ito-tsumadori-odoshi*. It was very popular during the later Kamakura and early Muromachi Periods (see Plate F).

A4: Dan-odoshi

These are two colours of lacing in alternating rows such as the *kurenai-shiro-dan-odoshi* pictured here. It was popular during the end of the Muromachi Period.

A5: Iro-iro-odoshi

This is the broadest variety of *odoshi*, having no really decided pattern. The only consistent feature is that there were at least three (preferably four) colours of lacing employed, and it was simply horizontal alternation. *Omodaka*, *tsumadori* and the like were not included as they actually had a fixed pattern, but *susogo* has at least once been termed as *iro-iro*. It became very popular during the last part of the Muromachi Period.

A6: Kata-shiro-odoshi

Kata means shoulder, and that is the mark of this pattern: the top two rows are of one colour, and all the rest are another colour. *Kuro-kawa-kata-shiro* (a

An armour representative of the late 16th century, a *hishinui-dô* is a variation on the *okegawa-dô*. Instead of using rivets, small Xs of lacing are used to hold the plates together. The *kabuto* has a crest based on the horns of a water buffalo. (Kôzan-dô)

common form) would have a double layer of white silk braid at the top, and the rest would be black leather. The pattern here is *hi-kata-shiro-odoshi*. Variations, such as *kata-aka* and *kata-kurenai*, were also common. An inverted form, *koshitori-odoshi*, became popular in the beginning of the Muromachi Period.

A7: Kozakura-odoshi

This is a printed leather lacing. Typically, the imprints of small cherry-blossoms (which is what *kozakura* means) would be either black or dark blue on tan, white, or yellow leather, although blue and red blossoms together have been seen. It was popular during the late Heian and early Kamakura Periods.

A8: Shida-kawa-odoshi

The fern is depicted on this lacing. There were two varieties: *shida-ai-kawa* and *shida-shiro-kawa*—the former is illustrated here, and the latter is a reversal of the colours. Lacing such as this seems to have required great skill to get the printed leaves to line up. It dates from around the Genpei War era.

A9: Fushinawame-odoshi

This lace also seems to have required skill to produce. After the multi-hued blue printed leather lacing was run through the holes, the complex pattern still had to match. It was most popular during the Nanboku-cho Period.

A10: Here we see a sample of lacing to explain some of the more common colours used by armourers. They are: *aka*, *hi*, *kurenai*, *kuro*, *midori*, *moegi*, *yomogi*, *kon*, *shiro*, *ki*, *hana*, and *cha*.

B: Tenkei no Ran, AD 940

The rebel commander Taira no Masakado and one of his officers are in conference before a skirmish against the emperor's forces.

Masakado (B1) wears an *ô-yoroi* which is only a few steps away from the ancient *keikô*. The lacing is direct vertical suspension (compare with that of Yoshitsune in Plate C), a hold-over from older armours, the pattern *omodaka-odoshi*. The helmet is fitted with gilt copper *kuwagata*, a prerogative of high rank in the early period. His single *kote* is simply padded cloth and has no defensive plates, its primary purpose being to keep the baggy sleeve of his *hitatare* (under robe) out of the way of the bowstring. (*Source*: armourer's model in Horyû-ji.)

These swords are typical of the late 16th century. The top is a **katana**, and the middle two the shorter companion sword, the **wakizashi**. At the bottom is a dagger called an **aikuchi**. Popular myth holds that the bottom blade was the ritual *seppuku* knife, but in truth samurai used whatever was handy. (Kôzan-dô)

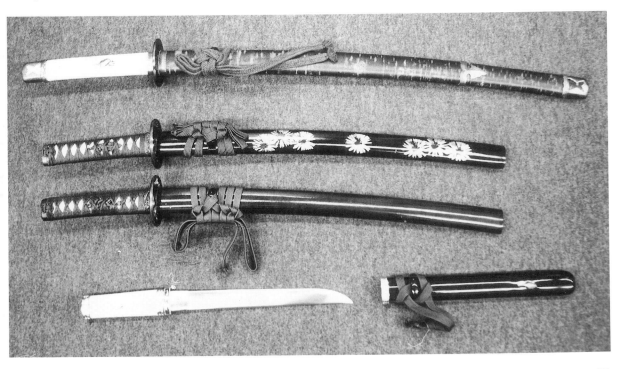

Masakado's lieutenant (B2) wears a similarly equipped *ô-yoroi* but his is laced with *kozakura-gawa-odoshi*. The complex arrangement of cords on the back of the armour serve to anchor the sode, and

This is actually a combination of two styles, the *niô-dô* and the *tachi-dô*. Called a *kata-nugi* (half-nude) *dô*, it represents the body of the wearer with half of the kimono worn loose to allow violent physical action such as fighting. Katô Kiyomasa wore such an armour. (Kôzan-dô)

will remain unchanged for centuries. Both he and Masakado have the tops of their caps pulled up through the hole in their *kabuto*, a very common style up to the 13th century.

The retainer (B3) with Masakado wears a *dô-maru* laced in natural leather. He wears a *happuri* to protect his head, but note the singular lack of any additional armour. (*Source*: battle scrolls.)

C: Ichi-no-Tani, 1184

The figures here are clad in a representative assortment of armour from the period. They are the tragic Genji commander Minamoto no Kurô Yoshitsune and three of his most loyal retainers: the giant warrior-monk Musashibô Benkei, Ise no Saburô Yoshimori, and Satô Tadanobu. The four are here depicted scouting the territory preparatory to the famous cavalry charge down the near-vertical wall of Ichi-no-Tani into the Heike encampment below. Note the changes in armour since the mid-10th century.

Yoshitsune (C1) wears the latest *ô-yoroi* and a *kabuto* with *kuwagata*. The choice of lacing pattern here, *murasaki susogo*, is taken from an account in *The Tale of the Heike*: 'On that day, Yoshitsune wore an armour laced in *murasaki-susogo* over a red *hitatare*. His helmet was fitted with golden *kuwagata*. His sword was gold-fitted, and his arrows were fletched in black and white. He carried a bow bound with rattan lacquered red, with a strip of white paper at one end to show he was the commander'. The *kote* actually belonged to him, and is one of a matching pair preserved in the Kasuga-Jinja; although he had a pair, here he wears only the left one in the traditional style. (*Source*: an armour of the period, excellently preserved, at Mitate-Jinja. Some fittings are different. It also is *murasaki-susogo*, but is not attributed to Yoshitsune.)

Tadanobu (C2) wears a hybrid armour which only seems to have been in vogue for about 50 years or so, called a *dô-maru yoroi*. It shares many features of the *ô-yoroi*, notably the boxy look and printed leather *tsurubashiri*, but closes like a *dô-maru* and has a greater number of *kusazuri*. The armour here is the one preserved in Oyamazumi-Jinja, said to have belonged to Yoshitsune. Note the simpler fittings compared to those of the *ô-yoroi*. The *kote* worn by Tadanobu are less ostentatious than Yoshitsune's but no more or less protective. Tadanobu wears both, this affectation only now becoming common.

Saburô (C3), a bit of a rustic, eschews *kote* and *kabuto* altogether for the sake of freedom of movement. His *dô-maru* is laced in dark purple leather, and like Tadanobu's *kabuto* and *kote* is typical of the middle-class samurai's gear. Dressing like this for battle was not unusual for the lower classes, but it was not common for direct retainers of a Minamoto general to do so. (*Source*: an armour preserved in the Oyamazumi-Jinja.)

Benkei (C4) wears armour, a *dô-maru* like Saburo's, under his monk's robe. He wears no helmet but does have a few metal plates sewn to the forehead of his cowl. For the battle he will wear a pair of *kote* like Tadanobu's under his robe, and perhaps *sode* as well. Usually, the *dô-maru* alone would suffice, typical of other warrior-monks of the period. His weapon of choice is the *naginata*, like many other famous monks of record. (*Source*: scroll paintings, armour in Oyamazumi-Jinja.)

D & E: The Mongol Invasion, 1281

This illustration represents an engagement between Japanese defenders and Sino-Mongol troops during the second attempted invasion.

The mounted samurai commander (D/E1) in this illustration wears an *ô-yoroi* only slightly different from that of Yoshitsune's a century earlier. The scales are slightly smaller, calling for a greater number of them and a greater quantity of lace. The *kuwagata* are of a newer, heavier pattern. Both the broad variety and the older, slender form would continue to be used side by side for years. His armour is laced in *shiro-ito-tsumadori*. A new addition to the armour is the *horo*, a cape-like garment worn suspended from the shoulders and tied loosely in at the waist. When riding at full gallop it billowed out, lending a terrifying appearance to the warrior. The *horo* would gain popularity in the 14th century and die out in the early 15th. In the mid-16th century (long after it had fallen into disuse) samurai wishing to restore the splendour of bygone days resurrected the *horo* as displayed in battle scrolls; but, ignorant of its true simplicity, they designed a wickerwork basket to support it so that even when standing still there was a huge billowing bubble of fabric on the warrior's back. The fur wrapping on the scabbard is a sign of rank, like the *kuwagata*. Whether the *horo* was also a sign of rank in the early days is still a

This *kawari-kabuto* belonged to Date Shigenori, cousin Masamune. The helmet crest is a stylised centipede. (Kôzan-dô)

matter of speculation. (*Source*: an armour in the Metropolitan Museum, New York.)

Figure D/E2 represents a low-class bushi in a short skirted *dô-maru*. For most of his rank, armours such as this or the *hara-ate* (only the fore-half of this style) was the full complement of armour worn. As samurai were beginning to wear the *dô-maru*, it was slowly being replaced for the lowest classes. His weapon is a *nagamaki*, essentially a long bladed sword mounted on a hilt of equal length to the blade. (*Source*: battle scrolls.)

The method of battle had changed greatly, especially with this new threat, so aristocratic samurai now fought on foot alongside the lower-class ones. D/E3 is a samurai wearing a *dô-maru*, preparing to take the head of a fallen invader. His *sode* are a very unusual type, shaped like a truncated triangle. The lacing is *fusube-gawa-odoshi*. (*Source*: an armour in Oyamazumi-Jinja.)

An invading soldier of uncertain rank (D/E4) is about to meet his end. Actual details of the Sino-Mongol armour during the invasion are sketchy; most scrolls seem to indicate that it was a brigandine

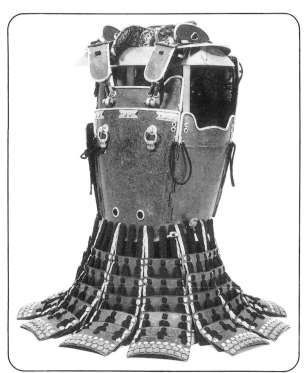

or studded coat of some form. Contemporary Chinese armour shows similar details but there are major points of variance with Japanese illustrations. It is likely that the discrepancy is due to the illustrator's unfamiliarity with the actual armours in question. It is assumed for purposes of illustration that the artists were close to the mark for the general troops, while the commanders wore the more ornate and efficient armours. (*Source*: battle scrolls.) D/E5, a Chinese commander.

F: Minatogawa, 1336
Here we see the royalist commander Kusunoki Masashige conferring with an attendant and a

Note the absence of *sode*, replaced by the 'small wings', on this unusually ornate *Sendai-dô*. The armour is black, with gilt fittings. Such armours were favoured by Date Masamune, who equipped his entire army with them. (Tôkyô National Museum)

(*Below*) The *Sendai-dô* opened to show the layout of the plates. There are eleven *kusazuri*, a very high number but not atypical with this style of armour. The brigandine collar also shows up fairly well, as do the *sode*—replacing *ko-hire*.

court liaison before entering the battle that would end his cause and his life.

Masashige (F1) wears half-armour, relaxing before donning his full armour and taking the field. This period marks the introduction of *haidate* as an armour feature. For the next hundred or so years they would be optional, but by the late 1400s *de rigueur*. Note that he wears his hair down and not in the familiar top knot. Before donning the *kabuto*, samurai usually let down their hair and wore an *eboshi*, a stiffened cloth cap. (*Source*: battle scrolls.)

The samurai (F2) wears a *haramaki* of a new form called a *kawatsuzumi-* (leather-wrapped) *haramaki*. Such armours, completely encased in leather, made their appearance during the Nanboku-chô Period. They were never very popular or numerous, but continued to be made until well into the Edo Period. No *sode* can be worn with this armour, but leather-clad *sode* made en suite with these armours were produced. This is also the period when underarm plates came into use. Previously, there was nothing but an occasional strip of padded leather attached to the tops of the scales, but now there is a solid plate designed to protect that vulnerable area. The *haidate* are of the second pattern popular in this period, and resemble baggy short pants with mail and metal plates on the front. This style would be common for a hundred years, but by the 1500s the simpler split-apron pattern replaced it, making it a rarity in the Sengoku Period. (*Source*: an armour preserved in Kongô-ji.)

The court noble (F3) wears a *haramaki* over his court robes, a common fashion for the civil/military élite at court. The armour would occasionally be worn under the robes as well. This style of dress, neither wholly civilian nor military, persisted even into the Edo Period. (*Source*: an armour preserved in a private collection, and a scroll.)

G: Gekokujô, c.1553

Gekokujô means 'the low overcoming the high', and is probably the single word which best describes the turbulent Sengoku Period. It was an age when those with no name or connections to greatness came from nowhere, and noble families fell into ruin. Hideyoshi is the perfect example: born of peasants, he rose eventually to rule Japan. This illustration, a common subject for Japanese artists of the period, depicts a group of ashigaru overcoming a noble samurai.

The samurai (G1) has been defeated and pulled from his horse by ashigaru. He wears a *dô-maru* laced in *iro-iro-odoshi* and a kabuto with a huge *mittsu-*

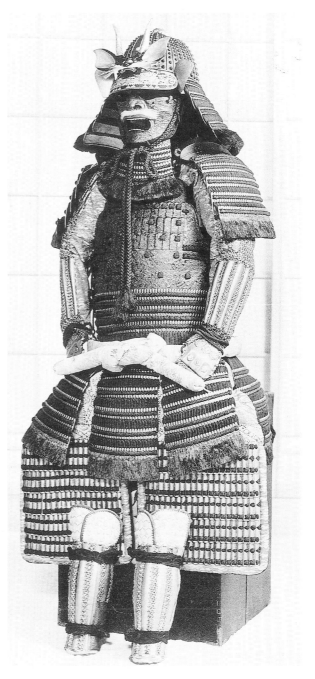

This composite of several late 16th century armour forms is very representative of the period. Styles were mixed during the Sengoku Era to create new variations (the *katanugi-dô* for example). The plates on the upper chest are made of *iyô-zane*, the middle of *hishinui*-set lames, and the bottom, *kebiki*-laced *kozane*. The armour is lacquered russet brown and gold with dark blue lacing. Bear fur ornaments the bottom plates instead of the usual cross-lace decorated plates. (Kôzan-dô)

Some armours were just plain gaudy. This one, a replica of a famous suit, has a gold axe on a red and black surface. The lacing is graded blue. It is a further example of the possible decorative variations afforded by the *hotoke-dô*. (Kôzan-dô)

H: Okehazama, 1560

Outnumbered 12 to one, Nobunaga makes the daring raid on the main camp of Imagawa Yoshimoto that will establish his reputation.

Imagawa Yoshimoto (H1) has removed his armour, which can be seen on a stand behind him. A member of one of the very ancient and aristocratic families, he still shows a fondness for the *ô-yoroi*. His aides had asked him not to remove his armour, but he complained that it was hot.

One of Nobunaga's soldiers (H2) prepares to plunge his *yari* into Imagawa. Like many of Nobunaga's men, he wears an *okegawa-dô* with a *sashimono* on his back bearing the Oda crest.

Nobunaga (H3) rides in. He wears a riveted-type *okegawa-dô* lacquered red, the rivets in gold. Usually, *okegawa-dô* were flush-riveted. An un-usually large Buddhist rosary is draped about his armour like a bandolier; several generals had a similar affectation (see Honda in Plate J/K), this perhaps being the Buddhist samurai's equivalent of the Crusader with a cross painted on his surcoat.

A low-rank Imagawa retainer (H4) attempts to attack Nobunaga. His armour is a *tatami-* (folding) *dô* of dozens of business-card sized metal plates connected by mail and sewn to a fabric backing. He wears only a *jingasa* with it.

I: Bad news, 1582

Tokugawa Ieyasu, visiting in Osaka, is informed of the death of Oda Nobunaga at the hands of Akechi Mitsuhide. Some of Ieyasu's chief retainers are present.

Ieyasu (I1) wears a rich *hitatare* with his *mon* as an overall design. This is a similar garment to that worn under armour by men of rank, but Ieyasu has fuller sleeves. The *hitatare* was the general day-to-day wear of the upper classes. He also wears a folded version of the *eboshi*. He stands on the *jôdan*, the dais used by daimyô when holding audiences.

The page (I2) is called the *tachi-mochi*, or sword-bearer; his duty was to hold the daimyô's sword in readiness during audiences. He wears a *kamishimo* (a matching *hakama* and *kataginu*) bearing the Tok-ugawa hollyhock mon. He wears his hair in the style of a youth who has not yet undergone the *gempuku* ceremony marking his entry, at the age of 16, into manhood, when he will receive the characteristic samurai hairstyle with the top knot.

kuwagata. (*Source*: An armour in Oyamazumi-Jinja.)

The ashigaru (G2), bearing his clan *mon* (crest) on his armour and *sashimono*, wears the new *okegawa-dô*. He wears a *jingasa* but no other armour.

A *hara-ate* of older, more traditional form is being worn by the ashigaru (G3), apparently of very low rank. He also wears a *kabuto* of an older, more ornate style, no doubt acquired in this very manner.

The ashigaru (G4) wears a *hara-ate* based on the *okegawa-dô*, and a rain cape of straw. This cape was commonly worn in colder or wet weather. His kabuto is the eight-plate 'helmet for a hundred heads', in common distribution in many armies.

Honda Tadakatsu (I3) also wears a *kamishimo*, the second most common apparel of the samurai. His *kataginu* bears his mon.

Chaya Shirijirô (I4), who first brought the news to Tadakatsu, wears *hakama* tucked into *kyahan*, and a patterned *kataginu*. He has just returned from Kyôto with the horrible news of the attack on the Honno-ji.

J/K: Sekigahara, 1600

The battle of Sekigahara was fought on 21 October 1600. With over 200,000 men in the field, it was the single largest battle ever to take place in Japan. The names of the participants read like a 'Who's Who' of Sengoku personalities. Both the loyalist army under Ishida Mitsunari and the faction under Tokugawa

Ieyasu had masterful commanders, some fresh from the Korean Campaigns of the late Hideyoshi period, and the outcome of the battle was anything but certain. This illustration shows some of Ieyasu's generals.

Ieyasu (J/K1) is shown here wearing one of his *nanban* (foreign) armours. This armour, preserved in the Toshogu Shrine, is one which he is said to have worn at Sekigahara. It is typical of Japanese adaptations of Western armour. All but the cuirass and the cabasset have been discarded, and even those have been altered to fit Japanese taste.

Honda Tadatsugu (J/K2), one of Ieyasu's bravest and most trusted retainers, wears his *nuinobe-dô* and *kabuto* with the antler-crest which had become his trademark.

A modern reproduction of Katô Kiyomasa's famous *naga-eboshi kabuto*. Although cap-shaped helmets were not uncommon, few were this large. (Kôzan-dô)

This acorn-shaped helmet is called *shii-nari*. It was not an uncommon shape for *kawari-kabuto*, but usually it was smooth-sided, not riveted. The helmet crest worn on the back is similar to one worn by Hideyoshi. (Kôzan-dô)

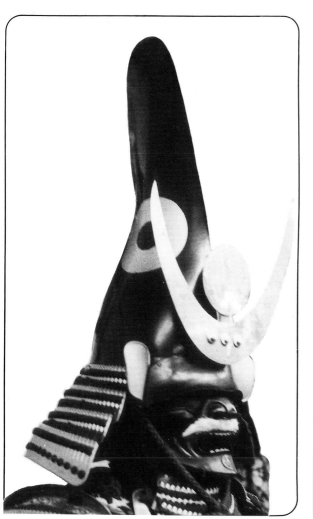

A modern reconstruction of the all-gold armour of Tokugawa Ieyasu, now preserved in the Tôshô-gu. The lacing is dark blue silk braid. (Kôzan-dô)

Date Masamune (J/K3), was not actually at Sekigahara, being at that time engaged in battle elsewhere in the Tokugawa cause. 'The One-Eyed Dragon' wears his favourite plain black *Yukinoshita-dô*, and a sword-guard as a patch to cover the eye he lost to a childhood disease.

Ii Naomasa (J/K4) wears a red *dangaie-dô*, and the gold-horned helmet that was his trademark. He equipped all of his army in red-lacquered armour because of its psychological impact on the enemy; they were known as the 'Red Devils'.

Kuroda Nagamasa (J/K5), one of Hideyoshi's commanders during the campaign in Korea, fought for Ieyasu at Sekigahara. He wears a *hishinui-dô*, and an 'Ichi-no-Tani' style *kabuto*, so named as the shape is supposed to bring to mind the cliff Yoshitsune rode down.

L: Ashigaru, 1600

Dozens of types of armour were worn by ashigaru. In fact, very few daimyô seem to have had a uniform supply, and many ashigaru used what they could find. This scene depicts a group from Sekigahara.

Ashigaru (L1) wears a *tatami-dô* of hexagonal plates with a similarly designed folding kabuto. This armour was very convenient and cheap, as well as extremely portable. By the Edo Period, even samurai lords were having ostentatious *tatami-yoroi* made for themselves, often in combinations with other styles.

L2 wears an unusual form of *okegawa-dô*: instead of having a hinge on the left side, the *dô* ties closed on both left and right. This means that the armour could also be worn as a *hara-ate*, with the back half not used. A similar armour is the *roku-mai-dô* ('six-plate cuirass'), which had four hinges and was

A rather fanciful rendition, this scroll painting shows Ieyasu and some of his generals. By and large the armours are combinations that never really existed, but they seem to be *kebiki*-laced *mogami-dô* made of scale rather than single-board lames, and occasionally graced with *tsurubashiri*. (Author's collection)

divided into separate back and front halves (hence 'six plate'), and tied closed at the left and right sides. They were cheap and simple, but never really popular.

Ashigaru L3 wears a *hotoke-dô* of the more modern solid-plate construction. He is an arquebusier, unlike the others, so a pouch for bullets has been attached to the waist of the *dô*.

Notes sur les planches en couleur
A Exemples représentatifs de modèles de laçage d'armure. A1 *Susogo-odoshi*—d'une seule couleur, allant de pâle à foncée, normalement blanche au sommet, puis jaune, avec ensuite les tons par graduation de la couleur. Une version inverse, de foncée à pâle, fut populaire lors de la guerre de Genpei. A2 *Omodaka-odoshi*—par supposition un motif de 'feuille', et un très ancien modèle. L'ordre des couleurs variait, mais si la couleur de fond était une teinte sombre, la première pyramide était blanche. A3 *Tsumadori-odoshi*—semblable à A2, mais un seul coin est visible. Populaire à la fin de la période Kakamura et au début de la Muromachi. A4 *Dan-odoshi*—deux couleurs alternant en rangées. A5 *Iro-iro-odoshi*—description vague d'un groupe de variantes, fondamentalement trois ou quatre rangs de couleurs alternés. A6 *Kata-shiro-odoshi*—les deux premiers rangs sont d'une couleur, le reste d'une autre. A7 *Kozakura-odoshi*—un laçage en cuir imprimé, typiquement avec fleurs de cerisiers noires, ou bleues ou rouges et bleues sur le cuir qui est tanné, ou blanc ou jaune. A8 *Shidakawa-odoshi*—un dessin de fougère exigeant une grande adresse pour l'assortir aux feuilles. A9 *Fushinawame-*

Farbtafeln
A Eine repräsentative Auswahl von Harnischen. A1 *Susogo-odoshi*—einfarbig, von hell bis dunkel abgestuft, in der Regel weiss an der Spitze, dann gelb und dann in abgestuften Farbtönen. Im Genpei Krieg war des umgekehrte Farbmuster gebräuchlich. A2 *Omodaka-odoshi*—offenbar ein 'Blatt'-Motiv sehr alten Ursprungs. Die Farbreihenfolge war unterschiedlich; war die Grundfarbe dunkel gehalten, so war die erste Pyramide weiss. A3 *Tsumadori-odoshi*—ähnlich wie A2, aber nur eine Ecke ist zu sehen. Während der späten Kakamura- und frühen Muromachizeit besonders beliebt. A4 *Dan-odoshi*—zwei wechselnde Farbreihen. A5 *Iro-iro-odoshi*—der Sammelbegriff für Farbkombinatinen, meistens drei oder vier wechselnde Farbreihen. A6 *Kata-shiro-odoshi*—die beiden oberen Farbreihen wurden einfarbig gehalten und der Rest war andersfarbig. A7 *Kozakura-odoshi*—bedrucktes Lederharnisch; gewöhnlich schwarz, blau oder rot und blaue Kirschblüten auf gelbbbraunem, weissen oder gelbem Leder. A8 *Shida-kawa-odoshi*—ein Farnmuster, das auf eine hochentwickelte Kunsthandfertigkeit bei der Gestaltung der einzelnen Farnblätter schliessen lässt. A9 *Fushinawame-odoshi*—

odoshi—un laçage en cuir imprimé aux couleurs multiples, créant des motifs complex. **A10** Couleurs courantes utilisées, respectivement: *aka, hi, kurenai, kuro, midori, moegi, yomogi, kon, shiro, ki, hana, cha*.

B1 La cuirasse de Taira no Masakado d'un modèle archaïque à un simple laçage à suspension verticale. Casque *kuwagata* doré, les cornes dénotent le haut rang. La protection du bras est un simple rembourrage. **B2** Le complexe laçage au dos de la cuirasse met fermement en place le *sode*, protection de l'épaule. Comme son maître, le dessus de sa coiffure est dégagée par le trou central du casque. **B3** Domestique portant la simple cuirasse *do-maru* et la protection de tête *happuri*.

C1 Yoshitsune porte la toute dernière cuirasse *o-yoroi* et un casque à cornes, avec une seule manche *kote*. Son costume et ses armes sont décrits en détail dans un ancien texte. **C2** L'armure hybride de Tadanobu est un style qui disparut rapidement, combinant les caractéristiques du *do-maru* et de l'*o-yoroi*. **C3** Exemple caractéristique d'armure de samouraï, plutôt campagnard, de classe moyenne. **C4** Le moine Benkei porte un *do-maru* comme C3 sous sa robe, et des plates de métal cousues sur son capuchon. La *naginata* était l'arme de choix pour de nombreux moines.

D/E1 La cuirasse comporte des plates plus petites et plus nombreuses que celles de C1, les cornes du casque sont plus lourdes que celles portées aux cours du siècle précédent. *Horo* ressemblant à une cape et qui se soulevait en vagues impressionnantes quand le samouraï était à cheval, est une innovation; on ne peut dire s'il s'agit d'une marque de rang au cours de cette période, comme les cornes du casque et le fourreau du sabre enveloppé de fourrure. **D/E2** Guerrier d'une classe sociale inférieure avec la nouvelle et sommaire armure *hara-ate* et le *nagamaki*, arme à manche. **D/E3** Les aristocrates combattaient plus souvent à pied à cette date. Notez les protections d'épaule, *sode*, peu courantes, de forme triangulaire. **D/E4** Les détails de l'armure sino-mongole portée pendant cette période sont basés sur des spéculations; les manuscrits présentent un genre de brigandine out de manteau garni de mailles. **D/E5** Commandant portant une armure chinoise plus ornée.

F1 Au repos vêtu de la moitié de son armure avant de s'habiller pour la bataille; notez les protections de cuisses, dites *haidate*, caractéristiques d'un samouraï à cheval à compter de cette période, mais restreignant trop les mouvements pendant le combat à pied. **F2** Cette armure s'appelait '*haramaki* à enveloppe de cuir'; elle s'attachait au dos. Les plates sous le bras commencèrent alors à apparaître. Les protections des cuisses sont du second genre, comme des pantalons amples et courts avec plates et mailles ajoutées. **F3** Un noble portant l'armure *haramaki* qui s'attachait au dos sur des robes courtes.

G1 Un samouraï vaincu portant la cuirasse *do-maru* et un casque avec les grandes cornes '*mittsu-kuwagata*'. **G2** Le fantassin Ashigaru, avec écusson de clan sur son *jingasa*, casque en forme de saladier, flamme et cuirasse à rivets 'aux flancs à forme baquet'—l'*okegawa-do*. **G3** Styles plus anciens d'armures *hara-ate* et de casques *kabuto*, probablement pillés sur le champ de bataille. **G4** Il porte une cuirasse *hara-ate* et une cape de paille contre la pluie ainsi qu'un casque bon marché composé de huit plates.

H1 L'armure de Yoshimoto, accorchée sur le support qui se trouve derrière lui est la traditionnelle *o-yoroi* d'un aristocrate conservateur. **H2** Soldat Nobunaga, avec cuirasse *okegawa-do*, et flamme *sashimono* portant l'armoirie Oda. **H3** L'*okegawa-do* de Nobunaga, vernie, avec les rivets dorés ce qui est peu courant; les rivets étaient généralement à tête noyée dans les cuirasses. Le large rosaire bouddhiste est un apprêt caractéristique. **H4** Suivant d'Imagawa, portant une cuirasse 'pliante' faite de nombreuses plates miniscules et de mailles sur un support en toile.

I1 La robe *hitatare* de Ieyasu, bien que les manches soient de forme plus ample, ressemble à celle que portaient généralement les hommes de rang sous leur armure; y est fixé son mon, ou écusson du clan. La coiffure, l'*eboshi*, est du type plié. **I2** Le page porteur de l'épée porte les cheveux d'un style convenant à un jeune qui n'a pas encore subi la cérémonie du *gempuku*. **I3** Le *kamishimo* était un autre accoutrement courant du samouraï; le *kataginu* porte l'écusson de Tadakatsu. **I4** Shirijiro porte son *hakama* replié dans le *kyahan* et un *kataginu* à motifs.

J/K1 Ieyasu porte l'une de ses armures 'étrangères', une cuirasse et un cabasset, transformés selon le goût japonais; celle-ci a survécu. **J/K2** Armure *nuinobe-do*, et casque avec bois de cerf en cimier de Tadatsugu. **J/K3** Masamune 'Le Dragon à un oeil', porte une garde de sabre en guise de couvre-oeil et son armure noire favorite, *yukinoshita-do*. **J/K4** Naomasa équipa toute son armée en armure rouge; le casque à cornes d'or était sa distinction personnelle. **J/K5** Voici l'armure *hisinui-do* et le style de casque nommé *Ichi-no-Tani* d'après la falaise que Yotshisune franchit à cheval.

L De nombreuses variantes d'armures portées par des fantassins ashigaru, car peu de nobles équipaient leurs hommes uniformément. **L1** *Tatami-do* faites de plates hexagonales et casque similaire—bon marché, portative et commode. **L2** Forme peu courante d'*okegawa-do* fixée fermement des deux côtés au lieu des charnières du côté gauche. **L3** *Hotoke-do* d'un modèle plus moderne et plus solide; il porte en tant qu'arquebusier un sac à balles à la ceinture.

---

buntbedruckter Lederharnisch mit umfangreichen Mustern. **A10** Die verwendeten Farben hiessen auf Japanisch: *aka, hi, kurenai, kuro, midori, moegi, yomogi, kon, shiro, ki, hana, cha*.

B1 Der Tairo no Masakodo Kürass mit altertümlichem Muster und einfacher vertikaler Schnürung. Ein vergoldeter *kuwagata*-Helm mit Hörnern gab Aufschluss über den hohen Rang. Die Armpanzerung besteht aus einfacher Wattierung. **B2** Die komplizierte Rückenverschnürung der Kürassverankerung des *sode*-Schulterschutzes. Wie der Lehnsherr trägt er die Spitze der Mütze durch die mittlere Öffnung im Helm. **B3** Ein Gefolgsmann mit einfachem *do-maru* Kürass und *happuri* Kopfschutz.

C1 Yoshitsune trägt das neueste *o-yoroi* Kürass und Helm mit Hörnern sowie einem einzigen *kote*-Ärmel. Seine Bekleidung und die Bewaffnung werden in einem alten Text beschrieben. **C2** Gemischte Tadanobu Panzerung wurde nur vorübergehend benutzt. Sie vereinte Merkmale des *do-maru* und *o-yoroi*. **C3** Eine typische Panzerung eines ländlichen Samurai aus der Mittelschicht. **C4** Der Mönch Benkei trägt einen *do-maru* wie in der Abbildung C3 unter seiner Robe Metallstreifen hatte man an die Kapuze genäht. Die *naginata* war bei vielen Mönchen die Bewaffnung ihrer Wahl.

D/E1 Der Kürass verfügt über weitaus mehr kleinere Metallstreifen als in C1. Die Hörner am Helm sind schwerer als im vorhergehenden Jahrhundert. Der umhangähnliche *horo* der beeindruckend im Wind bauschte, wenn der Samurai ritt, war eine neuerliche Hinzufügung. Ob es sich dabei um Rangabzeichen in dieser Zeitepoche gehandelt hat—wie der Hörner an den Helmen un die in Pelz gewickelte Schwertscheide-, ist unbekannt. **D/E2** Ein Krieger der unteren Klassenschicht mit dem neuen kurzen *hara-ate* Harnisch und der *nagamaki* Stangenwaffe. **D/E3** Die Aristokraten kämpfen nunmehr häufiger zu Fuss. Zu beachten ist der 'dreieckig' *sode*-Schulterschutz. **D/E4** Genaue Einzelheiten über das chinesisch-mongolische Harnisch, welches zu dieser Zeit getragen wurde, beruhen nur auf Vermutungen. Auf Schriftrollen existieren Zeichnungen über eine Art von Panzerhemd mit Beschlagnägeln versehener Umhang. **D/E5** Ein Kommandant, der einen geschmückteren chinesischen Harnisch trägt.

F1 Vor dem Kampf entspannt er sich, wobei er nur die Hälfte der Panzerung angelegt hat. Besonderer Beachtung gebührt dem *haidate* Oberschenkelschutz, der in dieser Periode von berittenen Samurais verwendet wurde. Der Schutz war jedoch zu beengend für den Erdkampf. **F2** Dieser Harnisch war ein aus Leder gefertigter *haramaki*. Der Verschluss befand sich am Rücken. Panzerung unter dem Arm tauchte nun langsam auf. Der Oberschenkelschutz gehört, wie die weiten kurzen Hosen mit zusätzlichen Schuppenpanzern und Rüstung, der zweiten Kategorie an. **F3** Über den Roben, die zu Hofe getragen wurde, wurde ein rückwärtig schliessendes *haramaki* Harnisch angelegt.

G1 Ein besiegter Samurai einen in *do-maru* Kürass gekleidet und trug einer Helm mit grossen *mittsu-kuwagata* Hörnern. **G2** Ein Ashigaru Fusssoldat mit Familienwappen auf dem schüsselförmigen *jingasa* Helm und der Fahne. Dieses Wappen befand sich ausserdem auf dem vernieteten 'tonnenförmigen' Kürass auch *okegawa-do* genannt. **G3** *Hara-ate* Harnische älteren Ursprungs sowie die dazugehörigen *kabuto* Helme, die höchstwahrscheinlich auf dem Schlachtfeld aufgelesen wurden. **G4** Er trägt ein *hara-ate* Kürass und einen Regenumhang aus Stroh sowie einen minderwertigen Helm bestehend aus acht Platten.

H1 Das Harnisch von Yoshimoto hängt auf eim Stand hinter ihm. Es handelt sich dabei um ein *o-yoroi*, das von konservativen Aristokraten getragen wurde. **H2** Ein Nobunaga Soldat mit *okegawa-do* Kürass und einer *sashimono* Fahne die das Oda Wappen birgt. **H3** Das mit Lackfirnis versehene *okegawa-do* Kürass ist aussergewöhnlich, da die Nieten vergoldet sind. In der Regel war der Brustpanzer mit bündig abschliessenden Nieten beschlagen. Der grosse buddhistische Rosenkranz war eine wurde nur zum Affekt mitgeführt. **H4** Ein Imagawa Gefolgsmann, der ein 'gefaltetes' Kürass mit kleinen Schuppenpanzern, die au verstärktem Material befestigt sind, trägt.

I1 Ieyasu *hitatare* Umhang, der zwar einen etwas volleren Ärmel hat, ist dem Umhang ähnlich, der im allgemeinen unter der Panzerung von ranghohen Männern getragen wurde. Auch hier ist sein mon oder Familienwappen zu erkenne. Bei der Mütze handelt es sich um die gefaltete *eboshi*. **I2** Der schwerttragende Page hat die Haarfrisur eines Jugendlichen, der sich noch nicht der *gempuku* Zeremonie unterzogen hat. **I3** Das *kamishimo* war ein häufig verwendetes Kleidungsstück der Samurai. Das *katagino* birgt das Tadakatsu-Wappen. **I4** Shirijiro trägt das *hakama* den in *kyahan* hineingesteckt und hat einen gemusterten *kataginu*.

J/K1 Ieyasu trägt einen siner ausländischen Brustpanzer, und zwar ein Küras und cabasset die dem japanischen Stil entsprechend geändert wurden. Dieser Harnisch kann man auch heute noch bestaunen. **J/K2** Ein Nuinobe-do Harnisch und ein Helm mit dem Geweihwappen der Tadatsugu. **J/K3** Masamun, 'der einäugige Drachen', trägt ein Schwertschild als Augenklappe und seiner schwarzen Lieblingsharnisch. **J/K4** Naomasa rüstete seine gesamte Armee mi roter Panzerung aus. Die Helme mit goldenen Hörner war seine persönliches Kennzeichen. **J/K5** Hierbei handelt es sich um das *hisinui-do* Harnisch im *Ichi-np-Tani* Stil nachdem Yoshitsune eine Klippe hinuntergeritten war.

L Die Fussoldaten von *ashigaru* trugen sehr viele verschiedene Harnische, da nur sehr wenige Adlige ihren Männern einheitliche Panzerung zur Verfügung stellte. **L1** Ein minderwertiger, tragbarer und bequemer *tatami-do* mit sechseckiger Schuppenpannzern und ähnlichem Helm. **L2** Eine ungewöhnliche Form eines *okegawa-do* beidseitig zusammengebunden, anstelle des Scharniers links. **L3** Ein moderner und robusterer *Hotoke-do*. In der Rolle des Arkebusiers trug er eine Patronentasche um die Hüfte.